You Might Be Too Busy If...

Spiritual Practices for People in a Hurry

GARY HOLLOWAY

LEAFWOOD
PUBLISHERS

To my friend,

Randy Harris

You Might Be Too Busy If...

Spiritual Practices for People in a Hurry

Copyright 2009 by Gary Holloway

ISBN 978-0-89112-626-3

Printed in the United States of America

Cover and Interior Design: Thinkpen Design, Inc., www.thinkpendesign.com

Leafwood Publishers is an imprint of
Abilene Christian University Press.

1648 Campus Court
Abilene, Texas 79601
1-877-816-4455 toll free

For current information about all Leafwood titles, visit our website:
www.leafwoodpublishers.com

09 10 11 12 13 14 / 7 6 5 4 3 2 1

CONTENTS

INTRODUCTION

You Might Be Too Busy If...

A Preliminary 10-Question Quiz to See If You Need to Buy This Book (and change your life)

1. If you balance your checkbook daily at 2 A.M....you might be too busy.

2. If the first item on your "To Do" list is "Make more 'To Do' lists"...then you might be too busy.

3. If you have more frequent flier miles than a major league baseball team...then you might be too busy.

4. If you cannot watch a movie at home with your family without folding clothes...then you might be too busy.

5. If you own a five-year daily planner and already have something scheduled for each day...then you might be too busy.

6. If people call your personal phone and hear, "I'm sorry but I cannot take your call at this time. Your call is important to me and will be answered in the order it is received. Average wait time is fifteen minutes"...then you might be too busy.

7. If you have written measurable goals and outcomes for your next vacation...then you might be too busy.

8. If you call in a delivery order for dinner while in the drive-through line for lunch…then you might be too busy.

9. If you've had to reschedule "quality time" with your kids at least three times in the last week…then you might be too busy.

10. Finally, if you feel guilty for wasting the time it took to take this quiz… then you might be too busy.

Scoring: If any of the above sounds like your life, then this book is for you. If you follow the practices taught in this book, you will find time to rest, reflect on your life, and enjoy those you love. This book will change your life.

If all of the above sound like you, paramedics are on their way.

If none of them sound like you, then you are already on the road to a well-ordered and restful life. This book can help you on that journey and can equip you to help others who need rest from their busy lives.

"Be still before the Lord, and wait patiently for him" (Psalm 37:7, RSV). What a strangely alien prescription the psalmist gives here for the fiercely active life of our time. We live in a culture that is not used to stillness; we are not schooled either in waiting or in patience. It has been suggested that we are not suffering as much from a decay of beliefs as from a loss of solitude. With the loss of solitude has come an inner alienation: "We are cut off outside ourselves."

Douglas Steere, *Dimensions of Prayer*, xv

ONE
WEARY TO OUR BONES

*Then, because so many people were coming and going that
they did not even have a chance to eat, he said to them, "Come
with me by yourselves to a quiet place and get some rest."*

MARK 6:31

Let us begin with confession. If you believe them, I ask you to say the following statements out loud.

"I am loved by God."

Try it again with more conviction.

"I am loved by God!"

One more confession.

"God is at work in me."

Again.

"God is at work in me!"

If we truly believe that a loving God is constantly at work in us, then that raises an important question.

Why are we so tired?

Hurried, Hassled, Busy, Tired

I am convinced that the biggest threat to our relationship with God and the biggest barrier to our quality of life is not immorality or secularism or humanism but simply this: we are too busy. Too busy doing good things. Too busy to do the best things. Too busy to live.

A typical day.

The alarm rings. You reach over and fumble to turn it off. Slowly you gain consciousness. Your first thought: "I wish I could go back to sleep."

But you can't. Instead, you drag yourself out of bed, throw on some running shorts, a shirt, socks, and shoes, and you go out to exercise. This is the only time in the day you can do it. You don't particularly enjoy running, but you do it.

Back to the house in time to start the coffee, take a quick shower, wake the kids and begin to get them dressed. After that you fix breakfast, pack lunches, kiss the kids good-bye, brave the cold, fight the traffic, and arrive at work ten minutes late.

It's not even 8 A.M. and you're already exhausted.

The day continues with meetings, deadlines, interruptions, phone calls, and emails. Work is repetitive and overwhelming. Finally, it's time to go home. You crawl home in the traffic, start supper, put some clothes in the wash, get everyone in to eat together (at least one day a week), drive Suzy to her basketball practice and Johnny to his piano lesson (on separate sides of town, of course), and arrive back at home to counsel your sister on the phone. Then back to get the kids and finally the nightly struggle of homework, teeth-brushing, and tucking-in. Sometimes there are a few moments to watch a game on TV or read a book, but most evenings you are catching up on work or house cleaning.

You fall into bed yourself, exhausted. Sometimes too exhausted to sleep.

Then the alarm rings and it starts all over.

And that's an easy day. The hard days are when the interruptions multiply. A visit to the emergency room. A huge last-minute project at work. The unexpected trip to care for your mother. The inner voice that wonders what all the busyness is for. Will it never end?

Finding Time

Sound like your life? We just don't have enough time. Time to really be with those we love. Time to think. Time to rest. Time to live.

Where can we find the time? Do we live for the weekends, when the pace is slower? But it's not. Saturdays are morning practices, mowing the grass, home repairs, and the inevitable party or dinner to plan or attend. Sundays? You've got to be kidding. By the time you get yourself and the kids ready for church, arrive late, get through the service without much hassle, then out to lunch, you are already exhausted. Sunday afternoons you do all the things you couldn't get to on Saturday. Sunday nights you

> In our culture we do not trust time. We try to defy time. We steal time, kill time. We want to control the flow of events, instead of trusting in a natural rhythm—instead of trusting that we can and will meet life as it happens.
>
> Gunilla Norris, *Sharing Silence*, 32.

help with homework and get ready for the workweek.

How about time off? Remember that last vacation you planned? Was it restful? All those weeks of finding the best deals, packing for the family, the stress of flying, trying to sleep in a strange bed. And the prices? You come home tired, in debt, and needing a vacation to recover from the trip.

Where can we find the time? Will a better To Do list or appointment calendar really help? Don't they just make us feel more rushed and busy? How about those time-saving appliances that were supposed to make our life easier? Have computers and cell phones simplified our lives and bought us time?

So we find ourselves increasingly busy and burdened year after year, until we retire, look back on our life, and realize we never found time to live. We never found time to listen to our children, to experience the joy of beauty, or to be with our God.

The tyranny of time in a life of busyness is well-expressed in the words of that heartbreaking song, "Cat's in the Cradle" by Sandy and Harry Chapin. You know the song. It is somewhat maudlin, but it captures what many of us experience. A father too busy for his son soon has a son too busy for his father. In the name of making a living, we lose what is most important in life.

Another Way

In short, our lives and our schedules are simply crazy. Why are we so tired, when God is at work in us? Many would answer, "Because we do so much for Jesus." In the name of serving God as Christians, we drive ourselves and others to distraction.

I know a woman, let's call her Martha, whose life is filled with church work. On top of family obligations and a full-time job, she feels compelled to volunteer to do anything and everything that needs to be done at church. She teaches children in class on Sundays and Wednesdays. She organizes the Ladies Day gatherings. She prepares food for every church occasion—potlucks, funerals, committee meetings. She has a weekly small group in her house. She directs weddings. She visits nursing homes and hospitals. She writes letters and cards. Sometimes she even bakes the communion bread.

> "Martha, Martha," the Lord answered, "you are worried and upset about many things, but only one thing is needed."
>
> MARK 10:41

And on top of all that, she feels she should be at every church activity even when she has no part in the planning or leading.

> God never guides us into an intolerable scramble of panting feverishness. The Cosmic patience becomes, in part, our patience, for after all God is at work in the world. It is not we alone who are at work in the world, frantically finishing a work to be offered to God.
>
> Thomas Kelly, A Testament of Devotion, 100

Martha often says she doesn't "do enough for the Lord." And she wonders why she is so tired.

Can you relate? Are you a Martha? Do you think you are not doing enough, even though you're going to church more? Is Christianity a burden, not a rest?

Are we doomed to a life of busyness in Christ, so busy that we do not have time to live? Or is there another way? Can there be a healthier, slower, more focused rhythm of life?

There can be.

Hear these words from John Ortberg:

> Not long after moving to Chicago, I called a wise friend to ask for some spiritual direction. I described the pace of life in my current ministry. The church where I serve tends to move at a fast clip. I also told him about our rhythms of family life: we are in the van-driving, soccer-league, piano-lesson, school-orientation-night years. I told him about the present condition of my heart, as best I could discern it. What did I need to do, I asked him, to be spiritually healthy?
>
> Long pause.
>
> "You must ruthlessly eliminate hurry from your life," he said at last.
>
> Another long pause.
>
> "Okay, I've written that one down," I told him, a little impatiently. "That's a good one. Now what else is there?" I had many things to do, and this was a long-distance call, so I was anxious to cram as many units of spiritual wisdom into the least amount of time possible.
>
> Another long pause.
>
> "There is nothing else," he said. "You must ruthlessly eliminate hurry from your life."[1]

It sounds good, but how can we ruthlessly eliminate hurry from our lives? Isn't that being lazy? If we are not wearing ourselves out in the service of God, then are we truly dedicated to him? Has anyone who accomplished anything for God ever completely eliminated the hurry and had a healthy rhythm of life?

There was one. One who not only lived this full life, but who now lives in us. We will look at his life in the next chapter.

Looking Inward

1. Do you feel rushed and hurried, without enough time? If so, why is it that way? If not, how have you avoided busyness?

2. Have you shared your frustrations with the pace of your life with someone else—husband, wife, friend? Do they have the same frustrations? Do they see the frantic pace of your life or do you hide it well?

3. What are ways you have tried to find more time and get more rest? How are those working for you?

4. Are you ready to try another way?

Try This Week

At the end of each day this week, take just a few minutes to look back at the day. When did you find yourself frantic? When were you at peace?

Tools to Help

Not as "one more thing to do," but if you get a chance, get a copy of Thomas R. Kelly, *A Testament of Devotion* (San Francisco: Harper, 1941) and begin to read it slowly. This brief book is one of the greatest devotional books ever written.

....

[1] John Ortberg, *The Life You've Always Wanted* (Grand Rapids: Zondervan, 1997), 76-77

There is a way of life so hid with Christ in God that in the midst of the day's business one is inwardly lifting brief prayers, short ejaculations of praise, subdued whispers of adoration and of tender love to the Beyond that is within.... There is no hurry about it all; it is a life unspeakable and full of glory, an inner world of splendor within which we, unworthy, may live.

Thomas Kelly, *A Testament of Devotion*, 98

TWO
THE SECRET OF A RESTFUL LIFE

But Jesus often withdrew to lonely places and prayed.

LUKE 5:16

There was one who lived a centered life and yet accomplished all he needed. He was active and busy, but not hurried and fretful. He had a healthy rhythm of life that trusted in God for direction and power.

His name was Jesus.

You saw that coming, didn't you?

There are always problems when we Christians talk about Jesus. One is that the Jesus standard is way too high for us. We think, "Well of course Jesus lived a good life. But I'm not Jesus."

But we are Jesus. At least, in a sense. We are not asked to merely imitate Jesus, as if we could be like him if we just tried hard enough. Instead our relationship with Jesus is much more personal and much more dynamic.

We know the passages. "I have been crucified with Christ and I no longer live, but Christ lives in me. The life I live in the body, I live by faith in the Son of God, who loved me and gave himself for me" (Galatians 2:20).

15

"Therefore, there is now no condemnation for those who are in Christ Jesus" (Romans 8:1).

Christ lives in us and we live in him. Therefore when we look at the life of Jesus we are not facing an impossible standard, but looking at the life God gives to all who are in Christ. Our lives are like his because he lives in us.

Even when we accept that he lives in us, we face a second problem. His life seems so different than ours. We might think, "Well, of course Jesus had a restful life. He lived in an earlier, simpler time. He didn't have to deal with traffic, schedules, and cell phones. He wasn't as busy as we are."

The Busy Jesus

Oh yeah? Do you really think Jesus was less busy than you? Do you think it was easier in his time to make a living? Doesn't carpentry sound like hard work to you?

How about the ministry of Jesus? People were constantly demanding his time.

"Teach us."

"Heal us."

"Show us."

Still not convinced? Then let's look at a typical busy day for Jesus, described in the first chapter of Mark.

Jesus begins the day at Capernaum teaching in the synagogue. As one who teaches, I can tell you, it may look easy, but it's tiring! He is interrupted in the synagogue by a demon-possessed man. Jesus casts out the demon.

Now, I've never cast out a demon, but I've got to imagine it drained Jesus of some energy.

After a busy morning, Jesus goes to Simon Peter's house for Sabbath lunch. But there can be no Sabbath lunch because Peter's mother-in-law is too ill to prepare it. Jesus heals her from her high fever and she immediately gets out of bed and prepares the meal. All those in Capernaum hear of this marvelous deed and after the Sabbath ends at sundown, they bring their sick and demon-possessed to Jesus and he heals them. "The whole town gathered at the door ..." (Mark 1:33). Jesus heals them late into the night.

Doesn't that sound like a busy day to you? Have you ever felt like the whole town (family, neighborhood, church) is gathered at your door, demanding that you help them? Can you imagine how tired Jesus must have been after a long day of teaching and healing? Other stories remind us that when Jesus healed, power went from him (see Mark 5:30). How drained he must have felt after this long day.

So what does Jesus do after a long busy day? Does he take the next day off? Sleep in? Just suck it up and work harder?

No. He gets up earlier than anyone else, while it is still dark, and slips out to a solitary place to be alone with God. Why? Is it because Jesus was super-human and did not require the rest we do? Of course not! It is because he needed rest that he spent time alone with God. In those moments alone with his loving Father, Jesus received the energy and direction he needed to move on.

Does it sound like nonsense? Or a least, against common sense? When we are exhausted, frazzled, and burned out, don't we usually think we need more rest and fewer responsibilities? But Jesus knew the secret of a full, deep, quiet but busy life. That secret was time alone with God.

If you give this a try, making time to be alone with God, what happens to Jesus will happen to you. They will find you. Those people who want something from you will eventually catch up to you. Peter and the disciples find Jesus. They even seem to criticize him, saying "Everyone is looking for you!" (Mark 1:37).

Have you heard that before? "Where have you been?" "Everyone is looking for you." "You've got work to do." No doubt Peter expects Jesus to get busy in Capernaum; after all, he had a great healing ministry going on there. People were eager and receptive. He had work to do.

How does Jesus respond? "Let us go somewhere else—to the nearby villages—so I can preach there also" (Mark 1:38).

Our lives are being simplified because we are giving attention to only one Voice, and our Yes and No arise from that Center. We no longer rush puffing and panting through our jam-packed day, yet somehow we accomplish more.

Richard J. Foster, *Freedom of Simplicity*, 86

What has happened to Jesus during his time alone with God? He has gotten energy and direction for his life. After a busy day of work, he now is eager to go elsewhere. He is not torn apart by the many voices clamoring for his time. He knows what God wants him to do. So he focuses his efforts, instead of living an out-of-control, try-to-help-everyone, do-everything, exhausting life. This is the promise of time spent with God—energy, direction, focus, and rest.

Another Busy Day

But what happens when it is not a typically busy day, but a day of emergencies, frustration, and loss? Jesus had those days, too.

> When Jesus heard what had happened, he withdrew by boat privately to a solitary place. Hearing of this, the crowds followed him on foot from the towns. When Jesus landed and saw a large crowd, he had compassion on them and healed their sick.
>
> Matthew 14:13-14

Jesus gets some terrible news. His dear friend John the Baptist is dead. Not just dead, but murdered—beheaded by King Herod.

What do we do when the terrible news comes, the news we have dreaded? We want to be alone, with those closest to us, so we can grieve in peace. That's what Jesus wants, time alone with God. So he gets in a boat and goes to a solitary place.

But he's not allowed to be alone. A large crowd hears where he is going and they gather there. Sometimes when we most need and want to be alone with God, we cannot.

So what does Jesus do? He puts aside his own needs and wants for a while. Out of compassion he teaches and feeds the huge crowd, five thousand men plus women and children.

But then what does he do? I've never preached before more than five thousand people at once. If I ever do, I'll never let them go.

Yet that is precisely what Jesus does. He makes the disciples leave and he dismisses the crowd. Why? What could be more important than teaching the disciples? What could be a greater ministry than preaching to huge crowds?

Being alone with a loving Father. That was more important than discipling, a greater ministry than mass evangelism. Late at night, after a long emotionally tiring day, Jesus makes time to be by himself with God.

Why? Because in deep loss, he needed comfort. Drained by those he cared for, he needed strength. Facing opposition, he needed courage.

If Jesus, the eternal Son of God, needed time alone with his Father, how much more do we. We are tired, frazzled, burned out because we have not learned the secret of Jesus. That particularly in the busiest of days, making time to be alone with God is not just one more thing to add to the schedule. It is the essential thing, the source of our power, peace, and plenty.

A Habit of Solitude

Jesus went to a lonely place to pray, that is, to grow in the awareness that all the power he had was given to him; that all the words he spoke came from the Father; and that all the work he did was really not his but the work of the One who had sent him.

Henri Nouwen, *Out of Solitude*, 21

In case we think Jesus only made time to be alone with God on his worst days, Luke tells us, "But Jesus often withdrew to lonely places and prayed" (Luke 5:16). Jesus developed a habit of getting away alone to spend time with God. That time alone is what kept Jesus in complete peace when surrounded by demands on his time and energy. It kept him from the crazy schedule and pace that many of us follow.

Can we have the same peaceful, focused, unhurried life as Jesus? Yes we can! The woman I called "Martha" in the first chapter has begun to discover that. In the busyness of her life, she habitually spends time alone with God each day. That short time shapes the rest of her day, slowing her down and keeping her focused. What she discovered, we all can discover. How we can is found in the next chapter.

Looking to Jesus

1. How was the life of Jesus counter-cultural when it comes to busyness?
2. Did Jesus accomplish enough? Should he have worked harder? Was his life as busy as yours?
3. What keeps us from following Jesus and accepting his rhythm of time?

Try This Week

This week when you feel particularly stressed and busy, try asking yourself, "What would Jesus do if he were in this situation? How would he find time and rest?"

Tools to Help

Take some time to slowly read and think about those two busy days in the life of Jesus (read Mark 1:21-39 and Matthew 14:1-23).

There is no grand, clear-cut path. But there are many little ways we can simplify our inner life during the day. These ways can rake the leaves of our flighty, cluttered lives to the outer ring of consciousness. The center can be left simple, open, spacious. Of course, the leaves blow back over the center with every gust of wind. And there are so many layers of leaves! Raking must be constant and long.

Tilden Edwards, *Living Simply Through the Day:*
Spiritual Survival in a Complex Age, 49

THREE
PRACTICES THAT BRING US PEACE

*A student is not above his teacher, but everyone who is fully
trained will be like his teacher.*

L U K E   6 : 4 0

Up to this point, we've had a good Bible study together on the life of
Jesus. Maybe you've found new things to think about. Now comes the chapter that can change your whole life.

Imagining a Better Life

It might seem like an outrageous claim, that your whole life can change.
Let us be clear. I am not claiming to be able to change your life. I'm not
even claiming that this book will change your life. I am not asking you to
change your life by your own effort (although the change will take coopera-
tion from you).

I'm not asking anything. God is. He is asking you to trust him, to let
him and Jesus live in you through the Holy Spirit. He claims he can and
will change your whole life, if you let him.

The first step in surrendering to the life God wants for you, a life rich and deep beyond your dreams, is to see what you can become. It begins with imagination. With a vision. Imagine a life that is peaceful, quiet, and fulfilling. Imagine your day being ordered by God. Not hurried and rushed. Not anxious and fearful. Imagine a life that is slower. A life that is rich. A life where there is time. Imagine finding time. Time to reflect on your life. Time to listen. Time to love. Imagine a life where we trust our little selves with God, who does our work in us. A life where Love is our center and all our actions flow from him.

> Life from the Center is a life of unhurried peace and power. It is simple. It is serene. It is amazing. It is triumphant. It is radiant. It takes no time, but it occupies all our time. And it makes our life programs new and overcoming. We need not get frantic. He is at the helm. And when our little day is done we lie down quietly in peace, for all is well.[1]

Receiving a Better Life

This better life we can imagine is promised by Jesus. He asks us a pointed question: "Are you tired? Worn out? Burned out on religion? Come to me. Get away with me and you'll recover your life. I'll show you how to take a real rest" (Matthew 11:28-29, The Message).

Then Jesus adds a puzzling statement, "Take my yoke upon you." Most of us have never seen a yoke except in a museum, but we know what yokes were for. You put the yoke on the neck of the oxen so they could pull the plow. Taking on a yoke does not sound like rest. It sounds like more hard work!

So why does Jesus say his yoke is easy? It's because he carries the yoke with us. A pair of oxen always worked together. Thus Jesus gives us deep and true rest because he works with us. He does our work for us. He asks us to work with him, not from our own strength, but with his. As we saw earlier, Christ lives in us and we in him.

> "Take my yoke upon you and learn from me, for I am gentle and humble in heart, and you will find rest for your souls. For my yoke is easy and my burden is light."
>
> Matthew 11:29-30

The secret of the easy yoke is not trying harder to be like Jesus but is letting Jesus live in us. But how do we do that? How do we make his life our own?

The answer lies in practice.

Practicing a Better Life

There is a great difference between trying and training.[2] My friend Randy Harris had not exercised regularly for years, but decided he wanted to do fifty push-ups on his fiftieth birthday. At first, no matter how hard he tried, he couldn't get past twenty or so push-ups. But after a few weeks on a regular exercise program, he reached his goal before his fiftieth birthday!

It is the same with every endeavor of life. No matter how much I want to (and I do), I cannot play the piano. I never took lessons! And obviously I don't want to play enough to learn and practice. Everything we currently do without thinking—walking, brushing teeth, tying shoes—was once new and awkward. We learned those things through practice.

If you want to raise your level of skill and become the best possible musician, practice won't be enough, says the world-renowned Israeli cellist Amit Peled.

The key to that elusive quality known as brilliance is the result of systematic practice—the kind of practice that is a daily, familiar routine that awakens your muscle memory and hones the basic skills of your artform.

From an article by Betsy Cohen in the *Missoulian*

This is the secret of the easy yoke. Jesus invites us to join him in certain practices. Traditionally these practices are called spiritual disciplines. I do not like the word discipline. It smacks too much of punishment for me. I understand that discipline just means consistency in training. But I prefer practices. We all know what it's like to practice—sports, music, theater, and other activities. "Practice makes perfect," we say.

But these practices are not about being perfect. They are not just one more thing to do in a crowded day. Instead they are the ways Jesus walks with us and we with him in a peaceful, restful journey to God.

Perhaps it is helpful to see these practices as tools. Tools are not ends in themselves. Imagine this dialogue with a stranger.

"What is it you do?"

"I'm very good with a hammer."

"Oh yeah, what is it you build?"

"I don't build anything. I just go around and hammer."

Wouldn't you think that strange? Tools have a purpose beyond themselves.

In the same way, the practices we share with Jesus are not ends in themselves. Jesus does not simply want us to pray better, read our Bibles more, and serve others more often. Instead, he uses these practices and others as tools to shape us into his image. It is essential to always remember that it is Jesus building us in the practices. They are not ways we build ourselves spiritually. They are never ways to make ourselves feel superior to others because we pray, meditate, or serve "better" or more than they do.

Beginning to Practice

Why is it some of us find it so hard to be disciplined in our spiritual practices? Maybe we think they are too hard. We've heard of monks and nuns. We may have known some super-spiritual Christians who pray twenty hours per week and serve another forty. We may think only those who have the time—single people, childless folks, the retired—can regularly live these practices.

Perhaps we have been overwhelmed by all the talk of spiritual disciplines. Some books list over forty different disciplines! How can we do them all? We are already too busy. Now you tell me there

> We too are yoked to the One who is trained. Our only task is to keep in step with him. He chooses the direction and leads the way. As we walk step by step with him, we soon discover that we have lost the crushing burden of needing to take care of ourselves and get our own way, and we discover that the burden is indeed light. We come into the joyful, simple life of hearing and obeying.
>
> Richard J. Foster, *Freedom of Simplicity*, 185

are forty more things I should do that I don't have time for!

Or it could be that we feel forced into the disciplines. It seems that everyone around us talks of their "quiet time" or the new book on spirituality they have read or the great retreat experience they just had. Meanwhile, we are having enough trouble just holding it together day by day, keeping our heads above water, trying not to drown in the sea of obligations.

If you can relate to any of these feelings, let me reassure you. These practices are for you. They are not for the spiritually elite, but for beginners like us. I have followed Jesus all my life. Still each day I begin again. These practices daily open my life anew to God. They take some effort and intention, but they are not too hard.

In the next few chapters, we will gently invite you into four (not forty) spiritual practices. These are the basic practices that Jesus does with us to build us into peaceful people. Enter them gently and slowly. Do not try all four at once. Practice them one at a time. Give them honest effort, but do not worry about getting them "right" at first.

This is not about doing things "right" but about a loving Father who wants us to try to walk with him. It is not about working harder, but about walking with Jesus each day. It is not about heroic effort, but about surrendering to the power of the Holy Spirit who works in us.

Most of all, these practices are about trust. When you begin, you might not feel restful immediately. You may regularly follow these practices for quite some time before you see results. It might even seem as if your life gets worse, not better for awhile.

No matter. Keep practicing. Practice in trust. Believe Jesus when he says that he will give you the rest you so desperately need. Know that he so much wants to give you a better life. He invites you to share his life—a life of joy and peace.

Looking Inward

1. How did you feel about practicing sports, music, plays, etc.? Did you enjoy practice? Was it just a chore? Did you think it was valuable?

2. How do you feel about following the practices of Jesus? Excited? Scared? Bored? Do you think it will be helpful or just one more thing to do?

3. Will spiritual practices always be an enjoyable experience? Why or why not?

Try This Week

Pick one thing you would like to do but do not normally do, and practice it for ten minutes at the same time each day. This does not need to be a "religious" activity, but can be anything—taking a walk, talking to your kids, working in the garden, calling old friends.

Tools to Help

You might find *Living God's Love: An Invitation to Christian Spirituality* (Abilene, TX: Leafwood, 2004) and Marjorie J. Thompson, *Soul Feast: An Invitation to the Christian Spiritual Life* (Louisville, KY: Westminster John Knox, 2005) helpful introductions to the spiritual practices.

---

[1] Thomas R. Kelly, *A Testament of Devotion* (San Francisco: HarperCollins 1992), 100

[2] For a more elaborate discussion of the difference, see John Ortberg, *The Life You've Always Wanted* (Grand Rapids: Zondervan, 1997), 45-62.

A serious and persevering discipline of solitude, silence, and prayer is demanded. Such a discipline will not reward us with the outer glitter of success, but with the inner light which enlightens our whole being, and which allows us to be free and uninhibited witnesses of God's presence in our lives.

Henri Nouwen, *The Selfless Way of Christ: Downward Mobility and the Spiritual Life*, 59-60

FOUR
DEEP SOLITUDE

After he had dismissed them, he went up on a mountainside
by himself to pray. When evening came, he was there alone.

MATTHEW 14:23

If we accept the invitation of Jesus to take on his easy yoke, then we must learn the secret of time that Jesus teaches, the practice of solitude and silence. In a life surrounded by distractions and noise, we must find ourselves and find God in solitude. Otherwise we will remain victims of a feverish busyness that simply rushes us from one thing to another. We will have a life full of activity but without the meaning that comes from quiet reflection.

> Solitude is the furnace of transformation. Without solitude we remain victims of our society and continue to be entangled in the illusions of the false self.
>
> Henri Nouwen, *The Way of the Heart*, 13

It is not enough to be busy. If that is all we have, then we will not find the time for the truly important things in life—family, beauty, rest, and happiness. We will be left at the end of our lives wondering where all the time went. In the words of an old Johnny Cash song, "When I've learned enough to really live, I'll be old enough to die." Or as Emily asks in the classic play, "Our Town," by Thornton Wilder, "Doesn't anyone ever realize life while they live it? Every, every minute?"

If we do not slow down and realize our life, then all of our activities are empty.

There is a way of realizing our lives. It is the way Jesus realized his. The way of solitude and silence.

Meeting God in Solitude

So solitude is good for us. We need it, just as Jesus needed it, to help us realize what life is really about. But that realization of life comes in solitude as a gift of God. Why practice solitude? Because we meet God there.

> And solitude is such a potential thing. We hear voices in solitude, we never hear in the hurry and turmoil of life; we receive counsels and comforts, we get under no other condition. For to be alone with Silence, is to be alone with God.
>
> Amelia E. Barr, *All the Days of My Life*, 294

Do not misunderstand. We do not make God show up. Our God is everywhere, surrounding us with his love. He lives inside of us all the time through his Holy Spirit. But although God is always with us, we are not always aware of his presence. This is what the spiritual practices or disciplines are all about. They do not manipulate God or make him show up. Instead they help us be more aware and mindful of his presence.

What God asks of us is nothing new. God's people have always met him in solitude. Moses is burdened, busy, and overworked with leading the Israelites. How would you like to be responsible for a people who often turn against the God who delivered them from slavery? Talk about a tough job! God himself is so exasperated with his people that he threatens to abandon them. "Go up to the land flowing with milk and honey. But I will not go with you,

> For the mercy of God is not heard in words unless it is heard, both before and after the words are spoken, in silence.
>
> Thomas Merton, *Disputed Questions*, 195

because you are a stiff-necked people and I might destroy you on the way" (Exodus 33:3).

So Moses is discouraged. What does he do? Does he simply soldier on, overworked and frantic? Does he quit? Does he try harder? Does he burn out?

No. He meets God in solitude.

Moses tells God he cannot lead the people unless God himself goes with them. God agrees. "My Presence will go with you, and I will give you rest" (Exodus 33:14). God then reveals himself to Moses, hiding him in the cleft of a rock while God's glory passes by.

How does Moses find rest in a busy life? He makes the time to be alone with God. God himself is with him. That is rest.

Elijah is discouraged. He has been busy working as God's prophet. Now he feels alone. No one listens. No one cares. "I have been very zealous for the Lord God Almighty. The Israelites have rejected your covenant, broken down your altars, and put your prophets to death with the sword. I am the only one left, and now they are trying to kill me too" (1 Kings 19:10).

Have you ever felt like Elijah? Tired and discouraged? Burnt out? The only one left? He even prays that he might die. "I have had enough, Lord," he said. "Take my life; I am no better than my ancestors" (1 Kings 19:4).

Do you ever feel that you've had enough?

But Elijah takes his deep discouragement to the right place. He does not hide his weariness, but he admits it to God. God leads him alone to a mountain. There Elijah experiences wind, earthquake, and fire. But God is not in those dramatic events. Instead God comes to Elijah quietly, in a gentle whisper. He gives Elijah strength and direction for his life.

Fear of Solitude

Moses, Elijah, Jesus. All found rest in solitude with God. That rest is not just promised to them but to us.

Why don't we accept that gift of rest? What keeps us from this blessing? We are distracted. We have bought into the lie of our culture that the answer to all problems is feverish activity. Even in the church, we push and plan and program ourselves to death. We let ourselves be distracted by good activities because we

> Accustomed to the veneer of noise, to the shibboleths of promotion, public relations, and market research, society is suspicious of those who value silence.
>
> John Lahr

lack trust. We find it hard to believe that our strength is found in quietness and trust in God, not in our plans, programs, and efforts.

Perhaps we are afraid of what we will find in solitude. There in the quiet, we come face to face with ourselves. Our fears. Our shame. Our brokenness. We might even be afraid of God. Afraid that in our solitude one of two frightening things will happen. Nothing. Or something. God might actually show up.

> It is in this solitude that we discover that being is more important than having, and that we are worth more than the result of our efforts. In solitude we discover that our life is not a possession to be defended, but a gift to be shared.
>
> Henri Nouwen, *Out of Solitude*, 22

But God's people have always found his presence to be frightening and reassuring at the same time. We know that "God is light; in him there is no darkness at all" (1 John 1:5). There are few things more wonderfully reassuring than light in a dark place. Yet no matter how good a housekeeper we are, we have all had the experience of light streaming through a window and revealing just how dusty our homes are. Every house looks clean in the dark. The light shows how dirty the place really is.

So it may be for us in solitude. God's light shines in places that we would rather keep dark and hidden. But his light is a cleansing light. In solitude with God, we let his light come in, to clean, to brighten, to comfort, and to guide.

Solitude is not always an enjoyable experience, but it is a good one. We must not let the lies of our culture, or our fears of what we might find in ourselves, keep us from this marvelous gift. The practice of solitude is where we find rest.

How to Begin

By now you might be thinking, "Solitude sounds fine for those who enjoy being alone, but I'm a people person. Solitude is not for me!"

You sound like my friend Mike Neill. Mike owns his own business, is on the road frequently, loves being with people, and can talk to a fence post! When introduced to solitude, he found it almost impossible. But he gave it a try. Now he will tell you that the practice of solitude has changed his life. He is still busy. He still loves being with people. But his busyness is not frantic. He is not hurried. He is centered. Not distracted. He is with people in a deeper way.

So, at first a call to solitude seems crazy in our busy over-scheduled lives. You may think, "If I don't have enough time to do what I'm supposed to be doing, how can I find time to be alone with God?" The answer is that we must learn solitude. Like all necessary tasks—walking, brushing teeth, tying shoes—it will not come easy at first.

The first step is simply to begin. Decide today that you will set aside a time—fifteen to thirty minutes—to be alone with God. Be realistic in your scheduling. If you are a mother of three young children or the CEO of a multi-national company, fifteen minutes might not be possible. But schedule a specific time that works for you. Perhaps early morning before your family awakes. Or late evening when they are in bed. Or a time during the day that you can pencil in "God" to your daily calendar.

If that seems impossible to you, then think of times you already have each day when you are alone—commuting in the car, lunch break at your desk, exercising, or other times. Can you intentionally turn those into times to be with God? While such multitasking is not ideal, it is a start.

Ideally you should have not just a set time, but a place to be alone with God. Jesus mentions going into your closet (Matthew 6:6). He himself liked to go into deserted places or up into the mountains to pray. Perhaps it can be just a favorite chair or room, where the family knows that is your place to pray and meditate undisturbed.

The important thing is not to obsess over place and time, but to start. Set aside a time each day to be aware of God's presence.

But what exactly should one do in that time? That's the focus of the next chapter.

Looking Inward

1. If Moses, Elijah, and Jesus found time to be alone with God, why can't we? What keeps us from the practice of solitude?
2. Do you find the idea of solitude and silence frightening? Why or why not?
3. In light of your life situation, how much time per day could you spend alone with God? When would work best for you? Will you give it a try?
4. When do you currently find yourself alone? Can some of those times be turned into times with God? What do you need to do in order to make those times of solitude?

5. Do you have a place for private prayer? Could you find or create one?

Try This Week

After prayer and reflection, write down the specific time and place that you will set aside to be alone with God each day.

Tools to Help

You might want to read the first chapter, "Time, Place, and Space, The Nuts and Bolts of How to Begin," in Mark E. Thibodeaux, *Armchair Mystic: Easing into Contemplative Prayer* (Cincinnati: St. Anthony Messenger Press, 2001). He gives great advice on setting aside a time and place for solitude.

Work is never separated from prayer. Rather, prayer frees us for carefree service of others, where we are no longer conditioned by the burden of necessity but always prepared for the novelty of grace. Just as silence conditions our words, prayer too conditions our works.

John Chryssavgis, *Light Through Darkness*, 31

FIVE
RICH SILENCE

But the Lord is in his holy temple;
let all the earth be silent before him.

HABAKKUK 2:20

Once you have made the commitment to set aside a time each day to be alone with God, the next question is, "What should I do in solitude?" There are many good answers. The basic answer is "nothing." Do nothing.

"Wasting Time" with God

For many of us, the hardest thing we can imagine is to do nothing. We have been taught from childhood to be busy, filling each moment of the day with activity. Our churches often teach us that to waste time is sinful. We should always be working for the Lord.

It takes great courage to fight the way we were brought up. Great courage to question what everyone knows to be true. Everyone knows that the more you work and the harder you try, the more you accomplish. Even in the spiritual life. That's why doing nothing is so wrong. Everyone knows that but God.

41

> The Lord your God is with you,
>   he is mighty to save.
> He will take great delight in you,
>   he will quiet you with his love,
>   he will rejoice over you
>   with singing.
>
> Zephaniah 3:17

God, our loving Father, knows that doing nothing with him is a rich and rewarding experience. That's why he often calls his people to quietness and rest.

God wants to gently quiet us, but when we have lives filled with a whirlwind of activity, we must wait for him to quiet us in solitude.

In solitude, God asks us to do nothing but wait quietly for him. But such waiting is hard. We prefer action. We find it hard to believe that God is doing something in us as we do nothing.

So in the time we have set aside for solitude, the most important thing we can do is nothing. We simply wait for God.

Active Waiting

But waiting does not come easy. We fuss. We fidget. We may begin to think of time with God like time in the dentist's waiting room. Not a pleasant thought!

So there are some things we can do to begin to quiet our hearts. One of those is to gently meditate on Scripture. This is not a Bible study where we get out

> I wait for the Lord, my soul w
>   and in his word I put my h
> My soul waits for the Lord
>   more than watchmen wait
>   the morning,
>   more than watchmen wait
>   the morning.
>
> Psalm

This is what the Sovereign Lord,
    the Holy One of Israel, says:
"In repentance and rest is your salvation,
    in quietness and trust is your strength,"
    but you would have none of it.
You said, 'No, we will flee on horses.'
    Therefore you will flee!
Yet the Lord longs to be gracious to you;
    he rises to show you compassion.
For the Lord is a God of justice.
Blessed are all who wait for him!

Isaiah 30:15-18

pen, paper, and commentaries. We are not looking to answer all the hard questions about the Bible. Instead, this is taking a small portion of the Bible, reading it slowly, then letting that word sink deeply into our heart. Perhaps a short phrase from the passage will speak to us. Take that word from God. Repeat it over and over. Let it be the word that leads you into silence before God.

Prayer is another thing we can do in our time of solitude with God. There are many good ways to pray. It is sometimes helpful to begin our time of solitude with prayers written by others. These set devotional pieces help to focus our thoughts on God. Of course, we can pray spontaneously with our own words, pouring out our hearts before God. As we pray in

> Let me understand the
> teaching of your precepts;
> then I will meditate on
> your wonders.
>
> Psalm 119:27

solitude, this is a good time to be aware that we pray with our bodies. One can bow, kneel, or lie prostrate before God in solitude without embarrassment. No one but God is looking! And our bodily posture does change how we pray.

A Vitalized Hush

But at least part of our time alone with God each day should be spent in silence. Bible meditation and spoken prayer should lead us into this restful waiting in silence upon the Lord.

This silence before the Lord is sometimes described as contemplative prayer. There are many ways to practice contemplative prayer. One that many find helpful is centering prayer. Centering prayer gives one a way to deal with the constant internal noise of our chattering minds.

One begins centering prayer with the intention of silently resting in the presence of God. As you begin, decide how long you will be in silence (ten minutes is good at the beginning).

> What deadens us most to God's presence within, I think, is the inner dialogue that we are engaged in within ourselves, the endless chatter of human thought. I suspect that there is nothing more crucial to true spiritual comfort than being able from time to time to stop that chatter, including the chatter of spoken prayer.
>
> Frederick Buechner

Sit comfortably. Become aware of your breathing. Gently let your thoughts go. Rest in the presence of God.

As you do this, you will become aware of noise. There will be external noises. You may find them distracting. Do not dwell on them.

More difficult is the internal noise of our own thoughts. Again, do not fight the thoughts but let them come or go. If you find yourself dwelling on a thought, then gently remind yourself of your intention of being silent before God. To help you in that reminding, centering prayer suggests you choose a prayer word, an appropriate word that reminds you of your intent to be silent before God. Father. Jesus. Spirit. Presence. Silence. Love. Peace. Or another word you choose. When you find thoughts getting in your way, say your prayer word to yourself to bring you back to silence.

> The mind wanders and the will falters again and again. Even the great masters of the religious life have confessed they were always liable to be invaded by the most frivolous thoughts during their meditations.
>
> Thomas F. Green

At first you might find this silent prayer frustrating. You might have to return to your prayer word dozens of times in ten minutes. That is fine. Each time you are committing yourself again to being with God. God will bless that intent.

The most important thing is the consistent attempt to be silent before

God. Do not be overly concerned with getting things right. There are many good ways to pray contemplatively and to be silent before God. Simply trust that God wants you to be aware of his loving presence with you.

What Happens in Silence

After a week of being silent before God for ten to twenty minutes a day, you will have a variety of experiences in the silence. You might feel physical or emotional pain. The bright light of God is sometimes painful to eyes accustomed to the dark. Resentments and bitterness that we thought we had overcome years ago might rise to the surface. What do we do with that pain? We give it up to God. We release it into his hands.

On the other hand you might feel euphoria or deep joy. You might experience a depth of peace you have not known. You might even drop off to sleep! No matter. God is pleased when his children fall asleep in his arms.

Most disturbing of all, you might feel nothing. After a week or a month or even years of daily silence, you may think nothing is happening. It all seems like a waste of time.

Mike Parker is a friend who struggled with silence. While others heard a word from God in silence, Mike did not. He wondered why God did not speak to him. He

A few basic methods are helpful in any mindfulness practice: the first is to have precise intention.... The second is to be allowing....The third is to be steadfast....The fourth is to be accepting of the fact that we cannot be flawless in our practice.

Gunilla Norris, *Sharing Silence*, 29-30

grew weary in the practice. But he persisted. Eventually God gave him this insight. In Mike's words: "God speaks to me all the time in the words I read, the thoughts I have, the things I see, and the conversations I have with others. I can no longer say God doesn't speak to me. It just takes some time for me to hear, see, feel, and comprehend the message. So next time we pray in contemplative prayer,

> Silence itself, of course, has no magic. It may be sheer emptiness, absence of words or noise or music. It may be an occasion for slumber, or it may be a dead form. But it may be an intensified pause, a vitalized hush, a creative quiet, an actual moment of mutual and reciprocal correspondence with God.
>
> Rufus M. Jones

I may still not have anything to share at the end of the prayer together but God will show me the answer when I'm prepared for it and when He thinks it's time. Now my prayer is not that God will speak to me with immediate words but that He will open my ears, eyes, mind, and heart to his message."

Silence may not result in an immediate word from God. Silence is also not about feeling. It is not about creating experiences. Feelings may come. If so, embrace them as gifts or face them with God as challenges. You might feel nothing. That is also fine. Silence is not our attempt to be spiritual or create spiritual experiences. Instead, it is an act of pure faith. We trust that God blesses those who spend time with him. We believe, even when we do not see, that God is working in us in the silence.

Therefore, in silence we receive from God. We receive deep peace. We receive strength for the day. We receive patience to wait for God to work.

Receiving from God may sound like a selfish act. It is not. Spending a few minutes each day doing nothing with God sounds like a waste. It most certainly is not. We should not feel guilt for what we receive from God in silence. What we receive is for our benefit. But it is also a great blessing to others.

> The more we receive from silent prayer, the more we can give in our active life. We need silence in order to be able to touch souls. The essential thing is not what we say, but what God says to us and through us. All our words will be useless unless they come from within—words which do not give the light of Christ increase the darkness.
>
> Malcolm Muggeridge, *Something Beautiful for God*

The purpose of silence is not merely to rest from the noise around us. It is not primarily a way to detach ourselves from our worries and distractions. Instead, in silence we are reattaching ourselves to the Source of our lives.

For in silence we receive words of wisdom and encouragement for others. In silence we receive the strength to love. Silence is the furnace that empowers our service to others. In silence we are centered on the real, the good, and the beautiful. It is not a withdrawal from the world, but an awareness of God. God within us. God around us. God in all things. God in all people.

It is in that awareness, that comes through silence, that we can begin to live in a deeper way. A simpler way.

Looking Inward

1. Is it difficult for you to be silent? Why?

2. Do you think God wants us to sometimes be silent in his presence? If so, why?

3. The Bible often encourages God's people to meditate on the Scriptures. What would that look like?

4. Will solitude and silence always be an enjoyable experience? Why or why not?

Try This Week

In your solitude time this week, take at least ten minutes for silence using the centering prayer method. At the end of the week, look back and reflect on that experience.

Tools to Help

If you would like brief daily Scripture readings and prayer to begin your time of solitude, try *Daily Disciple* (Abilene, TX: Leafwood Publishers, 2008) or the online daily readings at http://www.universalis.com and http://www.sacredspace.ie.

> It is in deep solitude that I find the gentleness with which I can truly love my brothers. The more solitary I am the more affection I have for them.... Solitude and silence teach me to love my brothers for what they are, not for what they say.
>
> Thomas Merton

A useful tool for meditation on the Bible is *The Meditative Commentary on the New Testament*, 12 volumes (Abilene, TX: Leafwood Publishers, 2006–2009).

To help you enter silence, look at C.W. McPherson, *Keeping Silence: Christian Practices for Entering Stillness* (Harrisburg, PA: Morehouse Publishing, 2002).

How different is the experience of Life when the Eternal Presence suffuses it! Suddenly, unexpectedly, the Divine Presence is upon us. Secretly, astonishingly, we are lifted in a plateau of peace. The dinning clamor of daily events—so real, so urgent they have been!—is framed in a new frame, is seen from a new perspective.... This world, our world, and its problems, does not disappear nor lose its value. It reappears in a new light, upheld in a new and amazing quiet power. Calm replaces strain, peace replaces anxiety. Assurance, relaxation, and integration of life set in. With hushed breath we do our tasks.

Thomas R. Kelly, *The Eternal Promise*, 30-31

SIX
THE SIMPLE LIFE

*Jesus answered, "It is written: 'Man does not live on bread alone,
but on every word that comes from the mouth of God.'"*

Matthew 4:4

Now you have spent at least a few weeks with a time of solitude. Perhaps you have had such a quiet time for years. Yet you still find your life cluttered, hurried, and busy.

What else can you do to find some rest?

Direction for simplifying our lives comes out of that daily solitude and silence. In prayer, meditation, and resting with God we find that we must (and can) let go of things that burden us. Some of those are literally things that we can do better without. The rest is inward stuff that we must let go. This chapter will focus on the tough but necessary job of outward simplicity. We give up stuff to make room for God.

Surrounded by Stuff

Think for a moment of all the stuff we own. A closet full of clothes. Clothes that constantly need washing. Sometimes ironing. Sometimes mending. Yet we have "nothing to wear." We need to shop for more clothes!

Then there are two or three or more cars we are paying for. You have to wash the cars. Maintain the cars. Fill the tank. Keep up insurance. Get the tag renewed.

Do you own a house? Mortgage payments. Insurance. Repairs! Replace the stove, refrigerator, heating system, roof, gutters. Ever noticed how everything seems to wear out at once?

In short, we have stuff. We spend our time looking at stuff. Buying stuff. Cleaning stuff. Insuring stuff. Protecting stuff. Fixing stuff. Worrying about stuff.

Some of us have so much stuff that we cannot keep it all in our houses. We have to rent storage space for our stuff!

And still we shop. No matter how much stuff we have, it's not enough. We must have new and better stuff!

What's wrong with stuff? Nothing in itself. God made the material world. Material things, stuff, are from God and meant for our good. But as with all

> Boredom with the ongoing grind of the real world leads to predictable responses: "Let's rent a video/go shopping/surf the Internet." Spiritual seeking leads to a bunch of uncomfortable questions: "Why am I bored? What void is this boredom telling me I need to fill? What will I discover if I just try to sit through my boredom?" Most days, most of us would rather rent a video than wrestle with our soul's hunger for meaning.
>
> Henry Sessions (1999)

God's gifts, this one can be misused. Desire for stuff soon becomes materialism. We expect too much from our stuff. We think buying something
new will make us happy. We take pride in owning what others cannot afford.
We let our stuff distract us.

The good things God made for us to enjoy soon become a burden. We
are weighed down by shopping for and caring for our stuff. Our God is a
God of freedom, not slavery. He wants to free us from our addiction to things.
He wants to lighten our load.

The Light Load of Jesus

The Word became flesh. Jesus lived in a material world. He had material
needs. He had stuff. But he learned the secret of the simple, restful life.

That lesson did not come easy for Jesus. He fasts for forty days and is hungry.
I guess so! I can't imagine the depth of his hunger. He sees stones. Perhaps they
look like loaves of bread. He thinks, "I can turn those stones to bread."

He could have. He had the power. What would have been wrong with
that? Is bread sinful? Is it wrong to eat? Doesn't God want his beloved Son
to have enough to eat? Would you starve your child?

But Jesus sees through his desire to turn stones to bread. He realizes it
is a temptation from Satan. As hungry as he is, he refuses to have his immediate needs met. He says, "'Man does not live on bread alone, but on every
word that comes from the mouth of God'" (Matthew 4:4).

Were these simply pious words Jesus made up on the spot? No. Jesus
had learned the lesson of simplicity by meditating on the Word of God.

Here he quotes the words of Moses to Israel, reminding them of what God had done for them.

> Remember how the Lord your God led you all the way in the desert these forty years, to humble you and to test you in order to know what was in your heart, whether or not you would keep his commands. He humbled you, causing you to hunger and then feeding you with manna, which neither you nor your fathers had known, to teach you that man does not live on bread alone but on every word that comes from the mouth of the Lord. DEUTERONOMY 8:2-3

We Americans are paralyzed by all our possibilities. We consider ourselves a tremendous nation because we can choose from a gigantic menu of consumer articles. Even Christians are ready to believe this sort of nonsense. When they do, they avoid traveling through the depths of the wilderness. Again, our enemy isn't pain, but the fear of pain.

Richard Rohr, *Simplicity, the Freedom of Letting Go*, 74-75

Israel and Jesus had to learn the same lesson we must learn. God provides our daily bread. He is a loving God who wants what is best for his children. But sometimes he wants us to be hungry. Why? Because he is mad at us? Because we have disobeyed? To punish us?

No. But because like every good parent, he knows that children must learn what and how to eat. Would you call someone a good father who let his children eat anything they wanted? Does a good mother let her children eat any time they want? No. They must learn to put food in the right place.

So God teaches us how to eat. More than that, he teaches us how to treat all our stuff. It's not that food, clothing, cars, houses, and other stuff is bad. It's that those things will not truly fill us. The only thing that truly satisfies our hunger is God alone. Thus, we find true life not in what we own, but in who owns us. Stuff will not make us happy. God does.

This lesson is particularly hard to learn in our culture. The advertising industry spends billions of dollars each year convincing us that purchasing their products will make life better. We are surrounded by voices urging us to give in to the temptation to have our immediate needs met. To resist that temptation requires great trust in God. We must not listen to those voices that make us afraid of the future. Can I find a profession that makes enough money? Can I afford to send the kids to college? Will we have enough to retire? Will the economy remain stable? Instead we must, like Jesus, learn to live lives of simple trust in God.

Lightening Our Load

How do we find that trust? Through prayer, meditation, and silence. But also by getting rid of some of our stuff. Jesus learned to rely on God for daily bread. He did not own a home, but had "nowhere to lay his head" (Matthew 8:20). He didn't have enough money to pay his taxes (Matthew 17:26-27). At the end of his life he is left with only the clothes on his back, and even they are taken away! (see Matthew 27:34).

"That's easy for Jesus," we might say. He was not married. He had no children. He didn't have a regular job. It's harder for us. We have mortgages, kids who need braces, and older parents to care for.

I don't think Jesus expects us to live exactly like he did. But he does want us to learn the secret of a simple, unhurried life. That will look a bit different for each of us. But for all of us, part of learning that lesson is getting rid of some of our stuff.

Why? Not to make ourselves feel bad because we don't have what we want. Not to feel superior to other "materialistic" people. We give up some stuff to lighten our loads. Our stuff has become a burden, keeping us from a better life. Giving it up is liberation! We are not giving up what we want and need, but laying aside what weighs us down.

How do we start? Go through your house room by room. Maybe start with the closets. Are there clothes there you wouldn't be caught dead in? Clothes you have not worn for years? Throw them out or give them to charity. Next, go to the garage. Are there tools you do not use? Get rid of them. Exercise equipment you never used? Maybe a neighbor wants it. Are there things in the rest of your home that you can do without? Give them away. Throughout this process the main rule is, "When in doubt, throw it out."

There are ways to make this practice easier and more regular. Every two months or so, my wife Deb and I get a call from a local charitable organization who will come by our house and pick up our stuff. That prompts us to look again for things we really do not need and can give away.

Still, giving away our stuff may be hard enough to do. Now comes the

harder part. Do not buy more stuff. Cleaning out the closets or garage is not an
opportunity for shopping. New clothes!
New tools! New gadgets! We must learn
to say no. No to all those advertisements
that promise health, popularity, happiness, security, and sex appeal if we only
buy more stuff.

> There are two ways to get
> enough: one is to continue to
> accumulate more and more.
> The other is to desire less.
>
> G.K. Chesterton (quoted in Richard J. Foster,
> *Freedom of Simplicity*, 100)

Enough is enough. Like Jesus, we must learn to say that God is enough.
We don't even need food, except as God gives.

But how much is enough? Many years ago I had a student who said
"Rich people live in three-story houses." He thought that because he lived
in a two-story house. Most of us are conditioned by our world to believe
that one more would be enough. One more donut. One more car. One more
necklace. One more raise. One more promotion.

That is nothing new. Adam and Eve are given every plant in the Garden
of Eden for food. Every plant but one. All they wanted was one more. So
they ate. And all the trouble started.

Fasting as Freedom

So what we most need to do is to change what we want. Human desires are
not bad. God created those desires. But when those desires are out of control they become bad. We must learn, like Jesus, to order our desires. To
want God first and only. And to learn that, we must give up some stuff. This

> Learn the wonderful truth that to increase the quality of life means to decrease material desire, not vice versa. Close your ears to the ads that bellow their four letter obscenities, "more, more, more!"
>
> Richard J. Foster, *Freedom of Simplicity*, 123

outward simplicity frees us from the tyranny of desire. It leads us into freedom.

In Scripture, freeing ourselves from the tyranny of desire is called fasting. We usually think of fasting from food, but it might help us more to fast from shopping, television, the computer, or other distractions. Fasting is not a way to lose weight, look good, or show others how religious we are (see Matthew 6:16-19). Instead fasting should turn ours hearts toward God and others.

Thus fasting is not merely an emptying. It is not making ourselves miserable so we can be holy. Instead it is a joyful and grateful filling with the goodness of God. In this outward simplicity of giving up our stuff, even sometimes giving up food, the Holy Spirit is working on us inwardly. God is working in us to simplify our hearts. We turn to that inward simplicity next.

Looking Inward

1. What examples of materialism, worry, and lack of focus can you give from your life, from other's lives, and from your church's life?

2. If simplicity marked the life of Jesus, is from God, and is good for us, why do we resist it? What keeps us from practicing simplicity?

3. What are some ways you let your possessions shape your sense of worth?

Try This Week

1. In your time of solitude this week, seek God's guidance on how to simplify your life.

2. Go through at least one room in your house and get rid of what you do not need.

3. Try a 24 hour fast from food (or a particular food), or from television, or from the computer, or from something else you think you need.

Tools to Help

Look at Richard Foster's classic, *Freedom of Simplicity* (New York: Harper, 1981), for profound wisdom on simplicity.

For practical help from a group who have practiced simplicity for years, see Catherine Whitmire, *Plain Living: A Quaker Path to Simplicity* (Notre Dame: Sorin Books, 2001).

> There is a realm of time where the goal is not to have but to be, not to own but to give, not to control but to share, not to subdue but to be in accord. Life goes wrong when the control of space, the acquisition of things of space, becomes our sole concern.
>
> Abraham Heschel, *The Sabbath*, 3

So many terrible things happen every day that we start wondering whether the few things we do ourselves make sense. When people are starving only a few thousand miles away, when wars are raging close to our borders, when countless people in our own cities have no homes to live in, our own activities look futile. Such considerations, however, can paralyze us and depress us.

Here the word call becomes important. We are not called to save the world, solve all problems, and help all people. But we each have our own unique call, in our families, in our work, in our world. We have to keep asking God to help us see clearly what our call is and to give us the strength to live out that call with trust. Then we will discover that our faithfulness to a small task is the most healing response to the illnesses of our time.

Henri Nouwen, *Bread for the Journey*, March 10

SEVEN
THE FOCUSED HEART

Blessed are the pure in heart, for they will see God.

MATTHEW 5:8

My friend Steve Davidson has a heart for the people of Honduras. Each year he makes several trips there with groups of college and high school students. When they return, the students always have the same reaction. "How can those people be so happy when they have so little?" These students can't imagine life without cars, electronics, and computers, much less

But godliness with contentment is great gain. For we brought nothing into the world, and we can take nothing out of it. But if we have food and clothing, we will be content with that. People who want to get rich fall into temptation and a trap and into many foolish and harmful desires that plunge men into ruin and destruction. For the love of money is a root of all kinds of evil. Some people, eager for money, have wandered from the faith and pierced themselves with many griefs.

1 Timothy 6:6-10

without electricity and running water. But they cannot deny the looks of joy on the faces of those they met in Honduras.

So does poverty automatically make one happy? If we get rid of enough of our stuff, will we constantly be joyous?

Of course not. Poverty is not the key to happiness. But what these students are shocked to find is that prosperity is not the key either. By practicing outward simplicity, lightening the load by getting rid of our stuff, our eyes are opened to the lies of our culture. Life is not about "more." It's about being content with what you have.

Inward Simplicity

So the practice of outward simplicity, freeing us from "stuff," is to allow God to simplify us inwardly. For some of us, this is our greatest battle. We are overwhelmed by demands on our time and emotional energy. We cannot say no to anyone who asks for our help. So our lives and schedules are out of control. We hurry to be late from one obligation to the next. When we are not frantically busy, we are obsessively worrying. We worry over children, spouses, finances, church, health, parents, and work. We worry over the past, the present, and (especially) the future.

But who will care for our children if we don't? Who will worry

> Still another step toward simplicity is to refuse to live beyond our means emotionally. In a culture where whirl is king, we must understand our emotional limits.... We are concerned not to live beyond our means financially; why do it emotionally?
>
> Richard J. Foster, *Freedom of Simplicity*, 91

about our wife or husband if we don't worry? Who will secure our future financially if we don't? Who will care for needy neighbors if we don't? Who will make the church what it should be if we don't?

God will. "Of course he will," we say. But then we live as if it is all up to us. We forget the simple truth that Jesus taught. Worry accomplishes nothing. "Who of you by worrying can add a single hour to his life?" (Matthew 6:27). That inward clutter of an unfocused, unsettled emotional life does more damage than good. By trying to do it all, we in fact do harm to ourselves and to those we think we are helping.

So how do we get rid of the inward "stuff" that clutters our hearts? We follow the path of Jesus. Surely no one cared more for others than Jesus did. We dare not accuse him of being lazy or unfeeling. Yet Jesus knew he had his limits. He could not do it all. He did not heal everyone, teach everyone, or worry over everyone. Instead, he had a single heart that focused on the calling and mission he

> To allow oneself to be carried away by a multitude of conflicting concerns, to surrender to too many demands, to commit oneself to too many projects, to want to help everyone in everything, is to succumb to violence.
>
> The frenzy of our activism neutralizes our work for peace. It destroys our inner capacity for peace. It destroys the fruitfulness of our own work, because it kills the root of inner wisdom which makes work fruitful.
>
> Thomas Merton, *Confessions of a Guilty Bystander*, 86

had from God. Jesus showed compassion, but he did not worry over those he could not personally help. Instead, he trusted God to show his loving care to them.

Jesus was also not distracted by what others thought he should be. The Pharisees and teachers of the law thought he should be stricter in his religious practices (as they understood strictness). The disciples James and John wanted him to send fire on the Samaritans and to make them his right and left hand men (Luke 9:54; Mark 10:35-37). Even his family wanted him to quit teaching because they thought he was crazy (Mark 3:21). But Jesus was not ruled by social conventions. He did not let others decide what he should do. He did not try to please everyone. He simply wanted to do the will of his Father.

Even Satan could not distract Jesus from his clear calling. He tries to get Jesus to focus on food, fame, and power. But in each case, Jesus refuses to lose his focus.

Jesus could have thought that he could do it all.

"I can turn stones to bread and still be the Son of God."

"I can jump off the temple, and everyone will follow me."

"I can rule all the kingdoms of the earth."

Instead he kept his eye on the prize. He had that single heart that wanted to do God's will. He put aside all the other good things he could have done to focus on his mission. His life was centered on his calling from God. He took the path of cross and resurrection. The path that leads to the rest that comes from faithfulness.

Purity of Heart

This same Jesus is at work in us, creating focus, vision, and purity of heart. He wants to give us that gift of a restful, purposeful, unhurried life. How do we receive that gift of inward simplicity? Through the practices of Jesus.

> Purity of heart is to will one thing.
>
> Sören Kierkegaard

We must practice saying "No." Jesus knew how to say no. He has a great preaching and teaching ministry in Capernaum. The whole town is at his door! Jesus withdraws to pray. Peter finds him and says, "Everyone is looking for you" (Mark 1:36). What Peter means is, "You have a successful ministry here in Capernaum. Why aren't you doing what you're supposed to do?" But Jesus has found direction for his life from prayer with his Father. "Let us go somewhere else—to the nearby villages—so I can preach there also. That is why I have come" (Mark 1:38).

Jesus did not let others set his agenda. He knew when to say "No" to demands and requests. But he said "No" in order to say "Yes" to the tasks God had for him.

Jesus, the Savior of the world, could say no to some of the good things people wanted him to do. So why do we have so much trouble saying no? Could it be that we have forgotten that there is only one Savior and we are not he?

> et us repudiate the modern
> access image of the person
> on the go," whose workload is
> double what any single person
> can possibly accomplish. Let us
> reject the delusions of grandeur
> that say we are the only ones
> who can save the world.
>
> Richard J. Foster, *Freedom of Simplicity*, 91

Some of us have a huge Messiah complex. If we do not do it, it will not get done. Or at least it will not be done as well. Of course, this impulse to help, to always say yes, stems from genuine compassion. People need us! But we sometimes forget who they really need. People need the Lord. He alone is their Savior. In all our busyness we intend to point people to him. But we soon forget that he is in control. He is working in us. He can help when we cannot. Our endless activity for Jesus can actually mask a lack of trust in him.

Saying yes to every request for help actually makes us less helpful. If we say yes to everything, we find ourselves overwhelmed, exhausted, and burned out. We find ourselves resenting those we claim to help. We embrace the call to compassion not as a joy but as a burden. We feel that all our hard work accomplishes little or nothing.

There is also a vision of the divine order which does not require each of us to take on everything. There is a sense that in a world under gospel order, or divine guidance, each person's appointed tasks would fit together organically, moving toward God's unknowable goals for the universe. There is a sense that we are not responsible for the outcome. We are responsible for faithfully discerning and performing our own personal parts in the process, leaving the outcome to God.

Patricia Loring

If we learn at times to say no, then we can say yes to our true calling. That is the key to inward simplicity.

But how do we know when to say "yes" and when to say "no"? It has much to do with "calling." In prayer and solitude Jesus found clarity about his calling. He learned from God where to go and what to do. So also with us. We must begin seeking the will of God in our times of solitude. We trust that God will guide.

> Jesus does not demand great deeds, but only gratitude and self-surrender.
>
> Therese of Lisieux

But how can we be sure of our calling? Through faith. By listening to God's Word in Scripture. Through silent, listening prayer. But there are other indicators. What type of service to others brings you joy? When you say "yes" to a request, do you immediately feel peace or feel regret? What gifts has God given you for service? How do others see God working in you?

We will look more at gifts, calling, and service in a later chapter. Now is the time to focus on inward simplicity. Purity of heart. Where Paul says, "This one thing I do" (Philippians 3:13), we say, "These dozen things I dabble at." Instead of being scattered and pulled in many directions, God calls us to a restful focus.

Practically, that means we must take stock of all the good things we do. What ministry saps your strength? Say no to it. Call up the one in charge and gently let them know you will not be a part. Who is it that wastes so much of your time? Avoid them. On the other hand, what service to others

> With our eye focused on Christ the Center, we are to live with glad and generous hearts. This is simplicity.
>
> Richard J. Foster,
> *Freedom of Simplicity*, 36

brings you great joy and satisfaction? Spend more time there.

Is this allowed? Can we say no and devolunteer? Not only is it allowed, it's required. God does not call us to overactivity and burnout.

This is a not a call to selfishness. It is not an excuse to be ugly to others. It is a godly recognition of our limits. Of course, there are times of emergency when we should serve in ways we are not suited. If you see someone bleeding by the side of the road, do not pass by, thinking "That's not my calling." Remember, the priest and the Levite did that (Luke 10:31-32). But do not become a victim to every "emergency" call from your church or your community. Serve where God has called you. Will one thing. Focus.

Gratitude and Joy

We cannot change the world. We can't even change one person, no matter how much we love him or her. If we try, we will only be frustrated. But God is changing the world. He can change the toughest heart. The amazing thing is that he invites us to work with him. Or better, to let him work in us. We work with him in focused, restful service. We do not take on the world's burdens, for he has already shouldered them. We do not fret over what we cannot do. We rejoice in what we can do, small as it might seem. We trust our little lives to God.

This recognition of our limits is not sad but joyful. We do not grieve over what we cannot do, but are thankful for what we can. We are not disappointed because we have not been given other gifts or callings. We are deeply grateful for where God has placed us. Serve those close. Husband. Wife. Children. Parents. Neighbors. Serve in joy. Let God take care of the world.

> Many things in life cannot be changed; we can only grieve over them. So long as we are no longer under the compulsion of wanting to change them, we have the freedom to change them. Then the change comes from a much greater depth— not from our anger, but from a place of integrity; not from a place where fear dwells, but from a deep trust; not from a place where self-right-eousness rules, but from wisdom.
>
> Richard Rohr, *Simplicity, the Freedom of Letting Go*, 74

Looking Inward

1. Do you find yourself living beyond your emotional capabilities? Are you constantly worried because you cannot help enough people?

2. Is your work a calling or just a way to make a living? Do you pray about your work? How can you make your daily tasks more enjoyable?

3. What area of life do you need to simplify the most? Are you willing to try? What would be the first steps to take toward that simplification?

Try This Week

1. Prayerfully take an inventory of all the activities you do. What brings you joy and energy? What drains you? What frustrates you? What causes

you the most worry? What would you like to let go of?

2. Choose one activity to drop in order to simplify your inner life. Do whatever it takes, no matter how painful, to drop it.

Tools to Help

The little book, *The Practice of the Presence of God* by Brother Lawrence (New York: Scroll Press, 2007), tells of how one man found inner simplicity in completing small daily tasks for God.

Perhaps the best tool to help in this area is a trusted friend who can help you see your gifts and calling. Find that friend and listen.

Church leaders like to think we are better than the normal folk; it is they who need to rest. We are exceptional; we are exceptionalistic. We think we are different—more energetic, less a part of creation, more a part of some fictional higher order.

Thus we make such a grand point out of obeying all the other commandments that we forget the one about rest. We become tired, grumpy, sometimes a little mean. The source of our trouble is ourselves: God gives us permission to rest. We refuse it. Thus, the first thing a leader can do to restore unto him or herself the joy of God's salvation is to remember that we are normal. We are not better than others by virtue of our calling; we are normal. Therefore, we not only may rest, but like others, we must rest. We begin Sabbath keeping by giving ourselves permission to be normal. From that permission comes the permission to rest. Without that permission, which comes from God through self, we will not be able to rest. With it we can begin to make the Sabbath connections.

Donna Schaper, "A Time to Rest: Sabbath Keeping for Leaders," *Lutheran Partners* (July / August 2001 • Volume 17 • Number 4)

EIGHT
A DAY APART

There remains, then, a Sabbath-rest for the people of God.

HEBREWS 4:9

Remember the healthy spiritual advice from an earlier chapter? "You must ruthlessly eliminate hurry from your life."

But it is easier said than done. Only regular practices of solitude, silence, and simplicity can make us so ruthless. But even those practices might not be enough. What a loving God has done for his people through the ages is to give them another practice to help. The marvelous gift of Sabbath. A day when we give up our busy striving. A day of gentle rest.

Why Sabbath?

We desperately need a day of rest. Unfortunately, many Christians have never been told that God intends Sabbath for them. Instead, like the Pharisees in Jesus' day, we would rather argue over how and when or even if we have to keep Sabbath instead of accepting it as a gift from God for our own good. Jesus reminds them (and us) what Sabbath is about:

Then Jesus said to them, "The Sabbath was made to meet the needs of people, and not people to meet the requirements of the Sabbath."

MARK 2:27 (NLT)

The word Sabbath means rest. God so much wants to give us this great gift of Sabbath, the gift of rest. It is a gift we and our churches need. We need constant reminders that God loves us out of grace, not because of what we do. Many of us believe we have embraced God's grace, but we are not willing to let God be the giver. We still think he will love and approve of us more if we work harder. Perhaps your church prides itself on being a grace church. But if your church is overworked, it's not a grace church! It is still trying to accomplish great things for God instead of receiving his gifts.

Sabbath reminds us that God is the one who provides. What is more, in Sabbath we are drawn into the very life of God. Why do we need Sabbath? Because God himself rested!

Churches aid the destruction of the Sabbath when they misunderstand or ignore its dimension of authentic rest and effectively turn it into another busy day of work. This happens when it is treated as a day of earning favors—from God and neighbor. If I go to church God will reward me. If I bring something to the potluck supper, my neighbors will think well of me. If I, as a pastor, plan many busy activities for everyone on Sunday, I am managing the church well.

Tilden Edwards, *Sabbath Time*, 72

Resting with God

We know that God rested from his work of creation on the seventh day. But what does that mean? Did God get tired? Does rest mean doing nothing? Has God done nothing since creation?

> What was created on the seventh day? Tranquility, serenity, peace, and repose.
>
> Abraham Heschel, *The Sabbath*, 23

Of course not! God has always been actively and intimately involved with his creation. We serve a God who works!

But in the Bible the work of God and the very life of God are sometimes described by the word "rest." Whatever God does is rest.

And he invites us into that rest! Now! Rest is not simply something we will enjoy with God when our life of work is done. God invites us to rest with him today. "Now we who have believed enter that rest, just as God has said" (Hebrews 4:3). The Book of Hebrews talks of all the ways God's people share in his rest. There is the rest after creation. There is the rest God gave Israel in the Promised Land. There is the rest David spoke of for God's people in his day.

But God's rest is not merely a thing of the past. It is for us today. "There remains then a Sabbath-rest for the people of God; for anyone who enters God's rest also rests from his own work, just as God did from his" (Hebrews 4:9-10). God gives us Sabbath to draw us into his very life. We participate in God's own nature, God's own rest. We share the unhurried, peaceful, serene life of God.

Resting with Jesus

Jesus kept Sabbath. He did not keep it as a ritual obligation. He did not keep all the rules that the Pharisees placed around Sabbath. But he did rest, worship, and serve on the Sabbath. He did not think God made us to keep Sabbath. He experienced this great gift of rest God made for his people.

But for Jesus, Sabbath was not a weekly obligation but a way of life. He not only rested on the Sabbath, but his whole life was restful.

As we saw in chapter 2, Jesus made time to rest in the middle of his busy life. He had a healthy rhythm of life—rest and solitude with God, community with his disciples, and loving service to others. Jesus was not frantic and worried. He did not burn out. He was focused on his purpose, his ministry, but he was not obsessed and over-worked. He knew how and when to rest.

He could even sleep when others were frantic. You know the story (Luke 8:22-25). Jesus is alone with the disciples in a boat. Some of us might think, "What a great opportunity to bond with the disciples. What a great opportunity to teach! Jesus had work to do in that boat."

Indeed he did. He rested. He slept. And when the storm came up and frightened the disciples, he still slept. Until they wake him. Then he calms the sea and asks the disciples, "Where is your faith?"

The work of Jesus in the boat was to

> Rest is what we do when we trust that forces greater than our own are circulating in the world, silently working for good. To practice Sabbath, or rest time, is to entrust our good work to the care of others.
>
> Paul L. Escamilla, *Longing for Enough in a Culture of More*, 77

rest. To sleep. In that work, he taught them (and us) a valuable lesson. Trust God. Rest with Jesus. He will care for you.

Remember to Rest

Are you convinced yet? Are you ready to start practicing Sabbath? Will you receive this gift from God?

If not, here is the clincher motivation. God commands it! "Remember the Sabbath day by keeping it holy" (Exodus 20:8). It's one of the top Ten Commandments.

Lately many Christians have become enthusiastic about posting the Ten Commandments in public places. I have a better idea. Let's actually do them. Not just nine, but all ten, including the Sabbath.

Strangely enough, I've known people who believe only nine of the ten were carried over into the New Testament. The one not applicable to Christians? You guessed it. The Sabbath! Which might explain why so many of us are tired!

Now it is true that Jesus nowhere commands his followers, "Remember the Sabbath." But he also nowhere says," I tell you not to murder." That doesn't mean it is now open hunting season on all those who irritate us. What Jesus does with the "do not murder" command is to get to God's original intent for the commandment. Jesus says, "You have heard that it was said to the people long ago, 'Do not murder, and anyone who murders will be subject to judgment.' But I tell you that anyone who is angry with his brother will be subject to judgment" (Matthew 6:20-21). God does not intend for us to hate someone's guts as long as we do not kill them. He wants us to even love our enemies.

As we have seen, it is the same with the Sabbath commandment. Jesus gets to the heart of it. "The Sabbath was made to meet the needs of people, and not people to meet the requirements of the Sabbath" (Mark 2:27 NLT). God commands Sabbath not just as one more thing we must do in a busy life. He commands it for our own good.

All of God's commands are for our good. He is not the great legislator in heaven thinking of new rules and regulations to make our lives more difficult. He is a loving Father who wants the best life for his beloved children. As a loving Father, he gives guidance for that rich and full life. He gives the gifts of commands. He gives Sabbath.

> What helps us most to live this way is knowing that the Sabbath is not a day off, but a day for. It is a day for re-learning the immensity of God's grace. Since we all need to learn that better, it is an extraordinary mercy that God didn't just suggest Sabbath keeping!
>
> Marva Dawn, "Sabbath: an Enormous Gift for the Congregation," *Lutheran Partners* (July / August 2001 · Volume 17 · Number 4)

Why Not Sabbath?

We need rest. God provides it. He invites us into the rest he enjoys. Jesus rested and calls us to rest. Our loving Father commands rest for our own good.

So why don't we rest? Why do we refuse to accept the gift of the practice of Sabbath?

Many reasons come to mind. Perhaps we are too much a part of a culture that measures our worth by what we produce. We have bought in to the illusions of power and control. We cannot give up control of our time to God, not even for a day. Instead we are deceived into thinking that busyness and fatigue are badges of honor, instead of signs of distrust.

We have to wean ourselves from the illusions of our culture. We have to let go and trust God as a child trusts its mother.

> My heart is not proud, O Lord,
>> my eyes are not haughty;
> I do not concern myself with great matters
>> or things too wonderful for me.
> But I have stilled and quieted my soul;
>> like a weaned child with its mother,
>> like a weaned child is my soul within me.
>
> PSALM 131:1-2

We do not accept God's gift of Sabbath because we forget who we are. We think we are what we do or what we accomplish. We forget that we are beloved children of God.

Do you love your children more when they succeed or when they fail? Do you love them more awake or asleep? Do you love them more when they are well or sick? Do you love them more when they are working or playing?

Silly questions. We love our children at all times. So God loves us. Because we are his beloved, we can rest.

Or perhaps we think Sabbath is for someone else. For those who are not as busy as we are. For single people. Couples without children. The retired. We have jobs and kids and schedules and responsibilities. We can't take a day off.

But some very busy people have found they must have Sabbath. I know a married couple. Both are physicians. They have three children less than five years of age. I cannot imagine how busy they must be! Yet a few years ago, they committed themselves to Sabbath. Now they will tell you it is one of the best decisions they ever made. "Sabbath changed our whole lives. We now have time to be with family and friends. It shapes every other day of the week."

Sabbath can be done by the busiest among us. Perhaps we have not received Sabbath because we don't know how. The next chapter will explore ways to accept the gift of God's rest.

Looking Inward

1. What examples of busyness and overwork can you give from your life, from other's lives, and from your church's life?

2. If Sabbath rest is from God, good for us, and necessary for Jesus, why do we resist it? What keeps us from practicing Sabbath?

Try This Week

1. In your daily time of solitude and prayer this week, seek God's guidance on Sabbath. How is he leading you to this practice? Ask him for strength to overcome resistance to a day of rest. Ask for wisdom on how to practice Sabbath.

2. If you live alone, find someone to talk to about Sabbath. If you do not live alone, take time to talk to your family. How could you practice Sabbath together? How might the practice bring you closer to one another and to God?

Tools to Help

Read Tilden Edwards, *Sabbath Time: Understanding and Practice for Contemporary Christians* (Nashville: Upper Room, 2003) or (for a Jewish perspective) Abraham Heschel, *The Sabbath* (New York: Farrar Straus Giroux, 2005). These books make a compelling case for Sabbath practice.

The Sabbath expresses the heart of the Good News, that God in Christ reveals an infinite love for us that does not depend on our works. It depends simply on our willingness for it, on our desire to turn to that Great love with our deepest love, through all our little loves. Thus observance of the Sabbath has an evangelical dimension. What better way to reveal God's love beyond our works than to stop our usual works and discover that Love is not withdrawn, but strongly visible for us?...In our simple Sabbath rest, doing nothing but appreciating the giftedness of life in God, we can reveal the Gospel to our neighbors in a demonstrable, non-aggressive, yet very challenging way.

Tilden Edwards, *Sabbath Time*, 91

NINE
ACTIVE REST

He makes me lie down in green pastures,
he leads me beside quiet waters, he restores my soul.

PSALM 23:2-3

We need a day to rest. A day to remember that God is in control. A day to play, walk, eat, and listen. We need a Sabbath.

But we are busy people. We can't imagine taking a day a week to do nothing!

But as we will see, Sabbath is not a day for nothing. It is a day with God. We waste time with him. And that is never a waste, but it is the practice we need to focus and maintain our active lives. It is no coincidence that Jesus talks about doing good to others on the Sabbath immediately after making his great promise, "Come to me, all you who are weary and burdened, and I will give you rest" (Matthew 11:28). Sabbath is not a day off, but a day for. A day for God. A day for others. A day for ourselves.

When Sabbath?

So how do we begin this practice? Begin by picking a day. Or if you just cannot bring yourself to rest a whole day, pick half a day.

> Understanding and cultivation of authentic Sabbath rest could go a long way toward saving churches from merely mirroring the human world of the law, where there is no appreciation of the unmerited grace that frees us for holy rest. The more this appreciation is present, the more relaxed and truly joyous church activities are likely to be.
>
> Tilden Edwards, *Sabbath Time*, 72

Hasn't God already picked a day? Doesn't Sabbath mean Sunday? I don't think so. For Israel, Sabbath was the seventh day or Saturday. Some want to transfer that to Sunday for Christians. It seems to me that fighting over which day marks us as Pharisees who would rather fight over the "rules" of Sabbath than practice it. Remember, God made Sabbath for us, not us for the Sabbath.

So choose what day works for you. Having said it does not have to be Saturday or Sunday, most of us have the weekend off, so one of those days makes sense for us. One suggestion is to begin Saturday night with a meal together with family and friends. Then have a restful evening together. Get to bed in time for restful sleep. Wake up slowly Sunday in time to prepare your hearts for worship. Experience restful, joyful worship. Spend Sunday afternoon in the restful activities described below. On Sunday night, begin the gentle transition back to the work week.

If weekends are not good for you (even preachers work on Sunday), then choose another day. The important thing is to be intentional about that choice. Do not let anything but a genuine emergency interfere with your Sabbath.

It is necessary to have a Sabbath day, but remember to take little Sabbaths every day. The time you spend in solitude and silence each day should bring deep rest. At other times of the day, particularly when you begin to feel frantic, just take a moment for deep breaths. For silence. For reflection. A Sabbath moment before an important meeting or task can make all the difference.

Stop!

What do we do on a Sabbath? The first, most important, and (for some of us) most difficult thing to do is to stop. Stop! For those of us whose usual speed is slow, stopping comes easy. For those who might be too busy, it is painfully hard.

We must learn to stop specific actions that are so much a part of our lives. It is not that those actions are evil. Indeed they are necessary. But for one day we stop and remind ourselves that the world will go on without our activities. Giving them up for a day may be difficult at first.

> "Be still, and know that I am God," really means in its full contemporary biblical setting: "Cease, stop, relax, Shut Up!...Have leisure and know that I am God."
>
> Robert Lee, *Religion and Leisure in America*, 262

> There is a realm of time where the goal is not to have but to be, not to own but to give, not to control but to share, not to subdue but to be in accord. Life goes wrong when the control of space, the acquisition of things of space, becomes our sole concern.
>
> Abraham Heschel, *The Sabbath*, 3

What do we stop doing on the Sabbath? First, we stop working. That does not mean we do nothing. It means we discover a different rhythm for a day. We stop doing what we do the rest of the week. We do not trade time for money. Most of our days are spent punching the clock or putting in the hours to make a living. There is nothing wrong with that. God expects us to provide for ourselves and our families.

However, on our Sabbath, we stop working to remind ourselves that it is God who provides. When we work hard, he is providing. When do not work at all, he still provides. Thus on Sabbath we try not to make or to spend money. Again, do not be legalistic about this. If you need some milk, buy some milk. But do not work. And don't spend the day shopping.

Not working may be difficult, but it is liberating. Imagine, a day without a "To Do" list. A day when we are free simply to enjoy time. A day when we do not fall prey to the demonic practice of "multitasking." One great bit of spiritual advice is "Be where you are." That is, be fully present in the moment. On Sabbath we can not only be where we are, but we can also do one thing at a time. We can be joyfully and fully engaged in whatever we do, moment by moment.

Our Sabbath should also be a day without worry. Some of us can imagine a day when we do not work, but we spend all our time worrying over the work that is piling up! But worrying accomplishes nothing. Even when we work, the work never ends. It always piles up! So on Sabbath, we truly rest from our work by letting God take care of things. For one day, we let him do our work for us.

That even includes church work. One reason many find it difficult to practice Sabbath on the weekend is that our churches get in the way. We schedule work days, outings, retreats, and meetings to "do the work of the church." Perhaps fewer scheduled church times would remind us of the true work of the church: to trust God alone. Sabbath leads to that trust.

People heavily involved in "church work" have found Sabbath a great blessing. Dean Barham is a busy pulpit minister at a 1,600-member church. One might think that ministers, particularly busy ones at large churches, make the time to practice Sabbath. Few do! Dean is an exception, having followed this practice for years. He says, "It isn't always easy to protect this time, but I look forward to it every week—I know the work and the demands will be

> The Sabbath is a day to cease striving. We no longer have to scramble after security by trying to be strong, to have all the answers or quick solutions, to be in charge of our time and schedules, to possess controlling authority, or to find easy gratification. What a relief it is not to have to try to be God, nor to create our future, nor to establish our security!
>
> Marva Dawn, *Keeping the Sabbath Wholly*, 30-31

there waiting when Sabbath is over, but this practice allows me to release that for a time to pray, play and be present with my family. With God's help, I pray that this becomes a state of my heart throughout the week, not just on that day."

Sabbath is also about being free from our stuff. As we are practicing simplicity daily, Sabbath calls for specific ways of avoiding the distraction of our stuff. One helpful tip is to have a Sabbath box where we liter-

> We don't stop very easily. Shabbat ceasing means not only to stop our work, but to stop worrying about the work and thinking that we're so important in the first place. How our lives are driven by our culture's need to accomplish! Similarly, churches clutter up their Sundays with "necessary" meetings and prevent their families from enjoying Sabbath rest together.
>
> Marva Dawn, "Sabbath: an Enormous Gift for the Congregation," *Lutheran Partners* (July / August 2001 • Volume 17 • Number 4)

ally or symbolically place all the things that can distract us from rest. For one day cell phones, wallets, email, headphones, televisions all go in the box so we can rest.

Look! Listen!

We stop on the Sabbath. But what do we do? Surely Sabbath is more than doing nothing?

What do we do on our Sabbath? We rest. Even nap. You may have been taught that napping is idleness and a sin. But remember

> In vain you rise early and stay up late, toiling for food to eat— for he grants sleep to those he loves.
>
> Psalm 127:2

In our culture...resting on the Sabbath is a revolutionary act. It is a day of "revolutionary tranquility." We liberate time (rather than space) as guerrilla soldiers. Stopping anxious productivity for a special time challenges the assumptions of a culture that would reduce us to production machines. The quality of Sabbath rest I have described challenges another temptation of the culture: to reduce us to leisure machines: consumers working hard to do what leisure industries tell us to do to keep us emptily busy and divert us from our deeper nature.

Tilden Edwards, *Sabbath Time*, 88

Jesus in the boat, sleeping through the storm. Sleep can be a prayer, a sign of trust in God. That's why some of us have trouble sleeping. We can't turn the world over to God for a few hours! On Sabbath we can rest and even nap because we put our day in the hands of God.

Sabbath is a time for play. Some of us have forgotten how to play. We need to watch children playing to learn how again. I'm not talking about the structured soccer league play we sometimes force on our kids. I'm talking about what children do if you leave them alone. They joyfully and restfully play. They don't do it to accomplish anything. They just have fun!

Discover what play is for you. Some find gardening restful. Some relax by jogging. Others of us see these activities as work. Play is what you enjoy. If you are a golfer, if you find it relaxing, then you can golf on your Sabbath.

What you must not do is "work on" your golf game. This is a time for rest, not frustration.

Walk on your Sabbath, but do not walk to get anywhere. Stroll. Meander. Wander aimlessly. Pay attention to the world around you. Look! Listen! Sabbath is a time to notice the beauty God has made. God himself is beauty. We joyfully worship him when we stop and wonder at what surrounds us. We marvel at the beauty we neglect most days of the week.

Rest. Play. Walk. Eat! Finally we found something we all like to do! But many of us have not tasted our food for months. Meals are just another hurried time we get through quickly to get to what is more urgent. Sabbath meals are different. They are not meant to be elaborate or gourmet. They are simple meals. But they are meant to be enjoyed slowly. Taste your food. Appreciate the variety of tastes God has made. Eat with others you enjoy.

For Sabbath is also a time to connect. We play, walk, and eat with others. This is why Sabbath time is so important to families and to friendship. We take the time just to be together. No hurry. No agenda. We are free to "do nothing" with each other and with God. And by doing nothing together, we connect on a much more profound level. We begin to appreciate others for what they are— amazing unique creations of

The Sabbath, thus, is more then an armistice, more than an interlude; it is a profound conscious harmony of man and the world, a sympathy for all things and a participation in the spirit that unites what is below and what is above. All that is divine in the world is brought into union with God. This is Sabbath, and the true happiness of the universe.

Abraham Heschel, *The Sabbath*, 32

God—not for what they can do for us.

We worship and serve on our Sabbath, but with renewed hearts. Sabbath worship is not an interruption in the day, but is part of its natural rhythm. It is a restful worship, whether at home with our families and friends, or with our larger church family. Service that grows out of Sabbath also has a different feel. We serve not out of obligation or superiority, but out of a deep sense of God's love for us. Such service is joyful and enjoyable. We'll talk about that in the next two chapters.

> When worship is rushed through amidst a harried, striving day, not only do we easily miss so much of the richness and depth of its celebrative heart, but we are often left with just another flat, burdensome time of work—just one more thing to do to get through and to get right with God.
>
> Tilden Edwards, *Sabbath Time*, 79

Imagine

Sabbath is stopping. Resting. Looking. Listening. Eating. Connecting. Worshipping. Serving.

Most of all, it is imagining. Imagine a life that is unhurried. Peaceful. Serene. Imagine a world where God does our work for us. In us. Imagine our only task to be following and receiving.

Perhaps the most famous Bible passage helps us imagine. Psalm 23. We know it. For many it is the funeral Psalm. But what if we did not wait until our funerals to experience the world this Psalm envisions. A world, a life, where the Lord is our Shepherd.

He leads. He restores. He prepares a table for us. He feeds. He protects. Even in the darkest valley, he is with us. We are not afraid.

Sabbath reminds us who we are. We are sheep. Sheep do not accomplish much. They are not frantically at work. The job of sheep is to follow the shepherd. On Sabbath we imagine the world as God intends it. He leads. We follow. He provides. We receive. He protects. We rest. We live in his house. Forever.

Looking Inward

1. Is having a Sabbath unrealistic? Are you willing to try? What would it take for you to have a weekly Sabbath?
2. What particular shape would your Sabbath take?
3. Do you see having a Sabbath as burdensome or liberating? Why?
4. What questions do you have about Sabbath keeping?

Try This Week

1. With family and friends, prayerfully make specific plans for your Sabbath. What day will it be? What will you do? Try to be specific enough so that you take your plans seriously, but flexible enough to where they do not become a "To Do" list.
2. Now do it. Have a Sabbath. Afterward, reflect with family on friends on what parts were a blessing and what might have been a burden. Adjust your Sabbath plans accordingly.

Tools to Help

These three helpful books give good practical advice on how to practice Sabbath. Lynn Baab, *Sabbath Keeping: Finding Freedom in the Rhythms of Rest* (Downers Grove: InterVarsity Press, 2005); Wayne Muller, *Sabbath: Finding Rest, Renewal, and Delight in Our Busy Lives* (New York: Bantam, 1999); and Norman Wirzba, *Living the Sabbath: Discovering the Rhythms of Rest and Delight* (Grand Rapids: Brazos Press, 2006). Do remember that reading about Sabbath should never take the place of having one!

The time is here when we must get deeper than our external programs of church activities in time, and recover the sense of the Eternal Order and the Eternal Love as underlying the whole of time. And Protestants have been supposing that religious work consists in *doing things for God*. We have been the active ones, planning what we think are the logical consequences, in action, of the Gospel of Christ. And we have wanted God to be the passive receiver of our offerings, our services. But the time is come when we must go deeper, and learn that *God is the active one*, and learn that we are meant to be acted through. We must go down deeper, and discover, as a *way of living*, not as a belief, how to be *pliant*, how to be *worked through by God*, who has become a living internal dynamic deep within us. Then indeed do we become active, as never before; but it is an activity that is *God-initiated*. It seems strange to say it, but the dynamic center of religion is in *God*, not in us; the world is in His Hands, not ours; the center of creative living is in *God*, deep down within us as a *lived fact*, not in our heroic…efforts to live for him.

Thomas R. Kelly, *The Eternal Promise*, 144-145

TEN
TIME FOR OTHERS

For who is greater, the one who is at the table or the one who
serves? Is it not the one who is at the table? But I am among
you as one who serves.

LUKE 22:27

We are busy people. Busy because we know there is work to be done. Perhaps it has been difficult for you to make time for solitude. Sabbath is even more difficult. How can we take a day to do nothing when so much needs to be done? All this talk of solitude, simplicity, and Sabbath may go completely against your nature and upbringing. Isn't it just an excuse for laziness? Shouldn't we be doing more (not less) for the Lord and for others?

Yes we should. But that service is not hurried and frantic. Indeed, all that you have begun to practice—solitude, simplicity, and service—is meant to make you more fruitful in God's service.

But for many of us, service is how we prove our worth. We serve because it makes us feel good about ourselves. But such "service" is condemned in

Scripture as "works righteousness." We do not serve to make ourselves pleasing to God. We serve because we know we are God's beloved. Out of that firm conviction we accept the free gift of adoption as God's children. And since we are his children, we begin to resemble him. We serve because God serves. Our work and service is his work in us.

A God Who Serves

What an amazing thought! The Almighty, the Creator, the God beyond our imagination makes himself our servant. And how much does he serve? The entire story of the Bible is of a God who gives. Who serves. Who works for us. Creation is service. He made us! He serves by making covenants with his people—Noah, Abraham, Israel. He humbles himself again and again to forgive and redeem his people. He loves us so much that he became one of us! "For God so loved the world that he gave his one and only Son, that whoever believes in him shall not perish but have eternal life" (John 3:16).

That Son of God, the Word made flesh, came not to be served but to serve. He knew he was God's beloved, so he was free to serve.

That attitude of joyful service is also ours through Jesus.

Each of you should look not only to your own interests, but also to the interests of others.

Your attitude should be the same as that of Christ Jesus:

Who, being in very nature God,

did not consider equality with God something to be grasped,
but made himself nothing,

    taking the very nature of a servant,

    being made in human likeness.

And being found in appearance as a man,

    he humbled himself

    and became obedient to death—

    even death on a cross!

Therefore God exalted him to the highest place

    and gave him the name that is above every name,

that at the name of Jesus every knee should bow,

    in heaven and on earth and under the earth,

 and every tongue confess that Jesus Christ is Lord,

    to the glory of God the Father.

PHILIPPIANS 2:4-11

Many of us live hurried, out-of-control lives because we do not let the serving Christ be in control of us. We rely on our own strength and wisdom as we work. But restful service to others through the power of God gives our lives calm, power, and integration. When we learn the secret of the easy yoke, that Christ works in us, then we experience the joy of hard work for others. "In everything I did, I showed you that by this kind of hard work we must help the weak, remembering the words the Lord Jesus himself said: 'It is more blessed to give than to receive'" (Acts 20:35).

A group of college students at our church experience the blessing of giving. At the beginning of the school year, the churches in our city "compete" to bring in the college students. They draw them with programs, parties, and free food. Our little church can't compete. Instead, our college students regularly go downtown to feed the homeless. As one student, Lori Burns, remarked, "Most churches feed the students, but you guys go out and feed others." She found that a greater blessing.

Why don't we experience the blessing of giving? Why do we find Christian service so hard and burdensome? Perhaps we are burned out because we rely on our own power. Perhaps service is a burden because we fail to practice prayer and meditation. Our lives may be too crowded for fruitful service. We need to simplify. Or maybe we need to serve less, that is, we need to find what work God has called us to and gifted us for.

However, it may be that we have simply been deceived about Christian service. We practice poor substitutes for genuine giving. We may first need to learn how not to serve.

Looking Good

It is OK to feel good when you help someone. It is not God's kind of service to help others in order to feel good. It is particularly deadly to our life in Christ to serve for the applause of others. Jesus himself made that clear:

> "Be careful not to do your 'acts of righteousness' before men, to be seen by them. If you do, you will have no reward from your Father in heaven.

"So when you give to the needy, do not announce it with trumpets, as the hypocrites do in the synagogues and on the streets, to
be honored by men. I tell you the truth, they have received their
reward in full. But when you give to the needy, do not let your left
hand know what your right hand is doing, so that your giving may
be in secret. Then your Father, who sees what is done in secret, will
reward you."   MATTHEW 6:1-4

Few of us will announce our service with trumpets. But we like to be
noticed for our service. However, such "service" is actually self-promotion.
We do not so much care for those
we help. We just like the feeling of
being noticed for our service. Such
"service" to others may actually be
harmful to them, because we treat
them as objects of our concern.
We patronize them. We know
what is best for them. What we
do not do is treat them the way
we want to be treated. The cure
for this "be rewarded" service
is to help others when no one
(perhaps not even those being
served) know it.

The trouble with the phrase "servant leadership", therefore, is that
though it moves away from inad-
equate views of leading others,
it still gets the order of the words
wrong. Leadership is the key term
and servant is the qualifier. What
we need today are not, as is often
suggested, more servant leaders,
but properly understood, more
leading servants.

Robert Banks and Bernice M. Ledbetter,
Reviewing Leadership: A Christian Evaluation of
Current Approaches, 110-111

There is a time to let our light shine, "that they may see your good deeds and praise your Father in heaven" (Matthew 5:16). The problem is when we do good deeds so that others will praise us. We soon grow addicted to that praise. Or we do good deeds so we can feel good about ourselves. But such good feeling does not last, because it is not rooted in God at work in us.

A more subtle form of this "feel good" service is the desire for Christian leadership. At first glance, such a desire seems right. Surely we should want opportunities to lead others for God. Surely we should pray that God will enlarge our territories for his sake. But this easily becomes selfish. I want to lead (because I know better than others what should be done). I want more opportunities for service (because it makes me feel

Our ambition is not leadership, but servanthood. Our task is not to grow leaders, but to make disciples who will follow Jesus. Our goal is not to get out there and get things done, but to listen and obey. Our call is not to exercise power, but to be faithful to our Lord and the way of the servant.

How God chooses to use his servants is his concern. We may be called to lead or to follow, to exercise authority or to submit, to turn our God-given gifts in one direction or another. But that is God's business. Our identity, our meaning in life, our sense of significance, and our self-worth are not to be based on the roles we fill, the power we wield, or the numbers we lead. We play to an audience of one, who loves us, affirms us, and uses us.

Steve Hayner, *World Vision Today* (Summer 1998), 5-6

worthwhile). I want to accomplish great things for God.

Service that is about us is not the way of Christ. It is not the selfless service God gives to his creation. Such "service" is not born out of our relationship with God. A relationship nourished by solitude, simplicity, and Sabbath.

Fixing Others

I have an embarrassing confession to make. When I was younger I thought I could fix others. If only these people would put their chaotic lives in my hands. I could straighten them up!

In fact, distancing ourselves from each other's pain is the hidden agenda behind most of our efforts to "fix" each other with advice. If you take my advice, and do it right, you will get well and I will be off the hook. But if you do not follow my advice, or do not follow it properly, I am off the hook nonetheless: I have done the best I could, and your continued suffering is clearly your fault. By trying to fix you with advice, rather than simply suffering with you, I hold myself away from your pain.

Parker J. Palmer, *The Active Life: A Spirituality of Work, Creativity, and Caring*, 85

As I've grown older, I've found I cannot fix anyone. As I sit and listen to the deep problems some face, my first thought is, "I have no idea how to make this better." The realization that I do not have answers is actually liberating. It frees me to do what I can do. I can love. I can listen. I can pray for them. But God alone knows what they need.

Yet many of us cannot resist that temptation to try to fix. What's wrong with trying to fix others?

It is arrogant. We assume that we understand what this person is going through. We think we know better than they do. We feel ourselves superior to them. How could they get in such a mess? Just a touch of common sense would have saved them. All they need is to listen to me.

It lacks compassion. By fixing, we distance ourselves from them. We are the strong. They are the weak. We have made good decisions. They make bad ones.

It is often racist and sexist. We think we can fix because we know what "they" are like. Isn't it just like a man (or just like a woman) to get into this mess. It is just like the (insert ethnic group here) to act this way.

It puts us in the place of God. We begin to think we run the world. Or at least we think we can run our lives and the lives of others. We forget that God alone is God. He alone knows what people need. He alone provides.

"Fixing" others puts us in bad company. We are like the Pharisees who tried to "fix" Jesus and his disciples. We are like James and John who wanted to fix the Samaritans by calling fire down on them (see Luke 9:54). We are like the older brother, who wanted to "fix" the prodigal son (Luke 15).

> What we usually learn, once we are there, is that there is no "fix" for the person who suffers, only the slow and painful process of walking through the suffering to whatever lies on the other side. Once there, we learn that being there is the best we can do, being there not as cure but as companion to the person who suffers on his or her slow journey.
>
> Parker J. Palmer, *The Active Life: A Spirituality of Work, Creativity, and Caring*, 83-84

Helping is good. "Fixing" is bad. But we help best by walking alongside others. We relieve suffering by bearing it. We help best by pointing to God, not to ourselves. Our advice. Our plans. Even our ministries.

Trusting God

All of these substitutes for genuine Christian service have one thing in common. They lack faith in God. It is God who serves. It is Jesus who is the suffering servant. We are asked not to serve for him, but with him. That trusting, restful service will be the focus of the next chapter.

Looking Inward

1. Do you often think of God as a servant? Are you comfortable with this picture of God? Why or why not?

2. Can you give examples from your own life of times you served to be seen by others? Can you give examples of letting your light shine so God is glorified? What is the difference between the two types of service?

3. What are some pitfalls of Christian leadership that you have seen in your life?

4. Do you try to fix others? Should you? If not, what should you do instead?

Try This Week

1. Find a way this week to help someone without their knowing it. Tell no one about that service. Reflect on your feelings around that service. Is it about your feelings?

2. In your time of solitude this week, take time to think about those times of service that brought you closer to God. What did you do? Could that indicate the type of gift God has given you for service?

Tools to Help

Three books that can help us recognize poor substitutes for Christian service: Henri Nouwen, *The Selfless Way of Christ: Downward Mobility and the Spiritual Life* (Maryknoll, NY: Orbis, 2007); Parker J. Palmer, *The Active Life: A Spirituality of Work, Creativity, and Caring* (San Francisco: Jossey-Bass, 1999); and Siang-Yang Tan, *Full Service: Moving from Self-Serve Christianity to Total Servanthood* (Grand Rapids: Baker, 2006).

We are significant terminals of Love and Power, ends of Love, we are also transmitting channels, means and ends of creative Love. Through us the hungry world must be fed. We dare not oppose the divine urgency. Great things may be done for men, for we do not do them; they are done through us. We do not carry the load in anxious balance. The living waters sweep through us to make green the fields of men. We are at peace. If we succeed, it is God who had succeeded, if we encounter defeat, then it is part of that strange resistance within History which God permits in a going world.

Thomas R. Kelly, *The Eternal Promise*, 36

ELEVEN
WORKING WITH GOD

For we are God's workmanship, created in Christ Jesus to do
good works, which God prepared in advance for us to do.

Ephesians 2:10

Those things we have begun to practice—solitude, silence, simplicity, and Sabbath—may at first seem to be focused on ourselves. We turn away for a while from the busyness of life to be alone with God. We focus on our relationship to him. We remember that "I no longer live, but Christ lives in me" (Galatians 2:20). That deep sense of who we are, beloved of God, frees us from our hurried, busy, frantic, unfocused lives.

But we are freed for a reason. Christ lives in us, so we live like him. We pour out our lives in service to others. This is not burdensome service that leads to burnout. It is the easy yoke of Jesus. We can serve restfully and joyfully because God works in us through Christ and the Holy Spirit.

Confident Service

Genuine Christian service thus begins with confidence in our relationship

When our ministry does not emerge from a personal encounter, it quickly becomes a tiring routine and a boring job. On the other hand, when our spiritual life no longer leads to an active ministry, it quickly degenerates into introspection and self-scrutiny, and thus loses its dynamism. Our life in Christ and our ministry in his name belong together as the two beams of the cross.

Henri Nouwen, *The Selfless Way of Christ: Downward Mobility and the Spiritual Life*, 16

with God. We are confident not because of who we are, but because of who God is. By his grace he has freely adopted us as his children. Say it again, out loud, with confidence: "I am loved by God!"

Convinced of that love, we are free to serve. This was also the experience of Jesus.

"Jesus knew that the Father had put all things under his power, and that he had come from God and was returning to God; so he got up from the meal, took off his outer clothing, and wrapped a towel around his waist. After that, he poured water into a basin and began to wash his disciples' feet, drying them with the towel that was wrapped around him" (John 13:3-5).

Jesus can humble himself to do the lowest act of service because he knows who he is. He does not serve from low self-esteem. Neither does he serve to gain points with God or with others. No. Instead, no act of service is beneath Jesus because he knows he came from and is returning to the God who loves him.

Since Jesus lives in us, we too serve from a profound sense of who we are, where we have been, and where we are going. Service is not ultimately about us. It is not completely about those we serve. It is all about the God who serves through Christ. By keeping that focus on God and his free acceptance of us, we can freely accept those we serve. Not as mere objects of our service, but as beloved children of God.

Prayerful Service

Prayer reminds us of God's love. That's why it is so important to pray as we serve. We are doing more than simply asking God to bless our ministry (as if we initiated our service to others). Instead we are asking God to draw us into his work of redemption. We are asking him to enable us to do what he is already blessing.

> Fill yourselves first and then only will you be able to give to others.
>
> Augustine of Hippo

Genuine Christian service grows from solitude and silence. Again, that is the way of Jesus:

> One of those days Jesus went out to a mountainside to pray, and spent the night praying to God. When morning came, he called his disciples to him and chose twelve of them, whom he also designated apostles....
>
> He went down with them and stood on a level place. A large crowd of his disciples was there and a great number of people from all over Judea, from Jerusalem, and from the coast of Tyre and Sidon, who had come to hear him and to be healed of their diseases. Those

troubled by evil spirits were cured, and the people all tried to touch him, because power was coming from him and healing them all.   Luke 6:12-19

> Prayer always leads us to the heart of God and the heart of the human struggle at the same time. It is in the heart of God that we come to understand the true nature of human suffering and come to know our mission to alleviate this suffering, not in our own name, but in the name of the one who suffered and through his suffering overcame all evil.
>
> Henri Nouwen, *The Selfless Way of Christ: Downward Mobility and the Spiritual Life*, 88-89

Note the rhythm of the life of Jesus. He spends time alone with God. He forms a community with others. Then he gives himself in service. He does not rush into ministry with his own power and wisdom. If he had, the demands would have overwhelmed him. He would have been hurried, frantic, and burned out.

Instead, Jesus leaves hurting needy people in order to be alone with God. This was not selfishness on his part. He is not merely tired of people. He leaves them for a time out of love for them. He knows that he can only truly love them with the power and love of God.

Solitude and silence prepare us for service. If we neglect them we can have no genuine compassion for those in need. With them, we have strength to love. Even the tough love necessary to help anyone over a lifetime.

Prayerful service allows us to help. It also reminds us of the only one who truly can help. God alone. Thus we not only pray before and while we serve, but we remember that prayer itself is service. There is nothing greater that we can do for others than to lift them up to God in prayer. Intercession is the greatest ministry of the church. Prayer is service. Prayer is helping. Prayer is work.

> Real prayer is more nearly work with God.
>
> Douglas V. Steere, *Prayer and Worship*, 13

Restful Service

Such prayerful service brings rest. We are free from the burden of ultimate responsibility for our service. It is God at work. That means we are called to be faithful in our work, not responsible for its effectiveness or outcome. Of course we want our service to be effective. We want good outcomes. We want people to be genuinely helped. But the results of our work are out of our hands. They are in the hands of God. We are called to trust those hands, not our own.

This kind of service is completely counter-cultural. We live in a culture that measures everything by quantitative outcomes. Christians and churches easily fall into this trap. We measure the "effectiveness" of our ministries with numbers. How big is the budget? How many were served? How many stayed off drugs? Out of prison? In a job? How many were saved? At what cost? At the early part of the twentieth century, Billy Sunday boasted that he had cut the cost of evangelism to $2 per soul!

But the Bible reminds us that God is in control, not us. He gives daily bread. He delivers from evil. He seeks the lost. He calls all people unto him.

When I think of the great works we are called to in our lives, works we avoid at peril of our souls, I think of works in which we cannot possibly be "effective." I mean such things as loving other people, opposing injustice, comforting the grieving, bringing an end to war. There can be no "effectiveness" in these tasks, only the commitment to work away at them, and if we judge such work by the standard of measurable outcomes, the only possible result will be defeat and despair.

Parker J. Palmer, *The Active Life: A Spirituality of Work, Creativity, and Caring*, 75-76

And he does not count the way we do. He leaves ninety-nine sheep to seek the one who is lost. He is not the God of scarcity and efficiency, but the God of abundance. When it comes to God's work, we cannot quantify the outcome. When we work with God, we merely plant the seed. We trust him for the harvest.

Such trust is radical freedom. We need not be anxious about whether we are serving "right." We trust our little lives and little acts of service with him. A cup of cold water in the name of Jesus still carried his grace. We are free to give up our own messiah complex to trust the true Messiah. We point others to him. He can heal. He can fix. He can save. That's not our job. Our job is to trust. To be faithful in our service. Such trust liberates us from self-judgment. As Paul found, it frees for joyful service.

So then, men ought to regard us as servants of Christ and as those entrusted with the secret things of God. Now it is required that those who have been given a trust must prove faithful. I care very little if I am judged by you or by any human court; indeed, I do not even judge myself.   1 CORINTHIANS 4:1-3

Some Christians serve as spiritual hypochondriacs, always overly concerned with the effectiveness of their ministries. Instead, let us focus on the faithfulness, not the "success" of our service. By doing so, we are actually freed to be more fruitful.

Small Service

Some Christians (out of good motives) want to accomplish great things for God. We ask God to enlarge our territory for his sake. However, our good motivations easily change into seeing ourselves as great heroes of service, accomplishing the work of God in hard and difficult fields. We forget that God alone is the hero! Service that does not focus on him but on our work is not true Christian service.

Other Christians become discouraged in serving others because our efforts seem so feeble. What we do is so small—a prayer here, a cup of cold water there. We are not as talented as others who serve. What good can we do?

> The world's work is to be done. But it doesn't have to be finished by us. We have taken ourselves too seriously. The life of God overarches all lifetimes.
>
> Thomas R. Kelly, *The Eternal Promise*, 31

Great good. Infinite good. Because we do not serve out of our strength but out of our weakness. It is that weak, small service, not daring "great things," that God blesses. In our little works, we rely on the power of God. Does sickness, age, lack of training, or lack of talent keep us from great service? No. For our weakness points to God's strength.

> But he said to me, "My grace is sufficient for you, for my power is made perfect in weakness." Therefore I will boast all the more gladly about my weaknesses, so that Christ's power may rest on me. That is why, for Christ's sake, I delight in weaknesses, in insults, in hardships, in persecutions, in difficulties. For when I am weak, then I am strong.   2 CORINTHIANS 12:9-10

And that is why such small undertakings as we make are important—far beyond their actual dimensions. They have an aura of the infinite about their heads. Viewed in the small, these undertakings are minute, against the world's sufferings, these little gestures of behavior and active concern. But they are acted symbols, media of communication of the life of the Spirit...and spoken to the world.

Thomas R. Kelly, *The Eternal Promise*, 84

Our little acts of service may seem like a drop in the bucket compared to the world's need. We want to save the world, but often we cannot help those closest to us. But God works best in little things. He creates the world out of nothing. Jesus takes a boy's small lunch and feeds five thousand people. The Spirit falls on a few at Pentecost, and through those few he turns the world upside down.

God can do more than we ever imagined with little acts of service. Just ask Linda Egle. As a flight attendant, Linda had often been to India and seen the struggle many women had with poverty there. Many cannot provide for their children. The situation forces children into child labor and prostitution.

So Linda decided to help in whatever way she could. She began a small business, Eternal Threads, to sell in America tote bags and cloth made by young women in India. God blessed her work, so that over 130 young women in India have a livelihood and an education.

No one is too small or too big to serve in God's kingdom. No service is too little. There is a place for us all.

> If you can't feed a hundred people, then feed just one.
>
> Mother Teresa

Gifted Service

If we serve with God's power not our own,

then we serve with the gifts God has given us. The Bible makes it clear that each of us has a gift for the sake of others.

There are different kinds of gifts, but the same Spirit. There are different kinds of service, but the same Lord. There are different kinds of working, but the same God works all of them in all men.

1 CORINTHIANS 12:4-6

Just as each of us has one body with many members, and these members do not all have the same function, so in Christ we who are many form one body, and each member belongs to all the others. We have different gifts, according to the grace given us.   Romans 12:4-6

Each one should use whatever gift he has received to serve others, faithfully administering God's grace in its various forms.   1 Peter 4:10

What is your gift? This is something different from talents or tendencies. It is the primary way God calls us to serve. The point here is not to be overly concerned with naming your gift. The point is that God provides what we need to serve others. Wherever you find opportunities to help. Whatever type of service brings you deep fulfillment. Whenever you feel a power greater than yourself at work in you. That is your gift from God. God at work in you.

God initiates the work. He plans it. He accomplishes it. And he invites us to share in it! This is the great joy of Christian service, not what we plan and do, but working with God and Christ through the Holy Spirit!

Receiving Service

We serve for God. We serve with God. We are served by God.

We help those in need, but we also are helped by them. Christian service is not simply a matter of helping the deserving poor or even the undeserving poor. It is discovering Jesus in the poor.

It is an amazing discovery, at first, to find that a creative power and Life is at work in the world. God is no longer the object of a belief; He is a Reality, who has continued, within us, His real Presence in the world....Too long have we supposed that we must carry the banner of religion, that it was our concern. But religion is not our concern; it is God's concern. Our task is to call men to "be still, and know that I am God," to hearken to that of God within them, to invite, to unclasp the clinched fists of self-resolution, to be pliant in His firm guidance, sensitive to the inflections of the inner voice.

Thomas R. Kelly, *The Eternal Promise*, 34

Do you remember the great judgment scene according to Jesus?

"Then the King will say to those on his right, 'Come, you who are blessed by my Father; take your inheritance, the kingdom prepared for you since the creation of the world. For I was hungry and you gave me something to eat, I was thirsty and you gave me something to drink, I was a stranger and you invited me in, I needed clothes and you clothed me, I was sick and you looked after me, I was in prison and you came to visit me.'

"Then the righteous will answer him, 'Lord, when did we see you hungry and feed you, or thirsty and give you something to drink? When did we see you a stranger and invite you in, or needing clothes and clothe you? When did we see you sick or in prison and go to visit you?'

"The King will reply, 'I tell you the truth, whatever you did for one of the least of these brothers of mine, you did for me.'"

MATTHEW 25:34-40

We have the great blessing of receiving Jesus in the poor. We come to those in need not as great heroes accomplishing wonders for God. No. We come as beggars, needing grace from those we serve. We come to find the face of Jesus in those we are called and privileged to serve.

It is disquieting to realize how little value I attribute to "the least of these," the ones deemed by our Lord to be great in the Kingdom (Matt.5:19, NIV). I have viewed them as weak ones waiting to be rescued, not bearers of divine treasures. The dominance of my giving overshadows and stifles the rich endowments that the Creator has invested in those I have considered destitute. I selectively ignore that the moneyed, empowered, learned ones will enter this kingdom with enormous difficulty.

Robert D. Lupton. *Compassion, Justice, and the Christian Life:*
Rethinking Ministry to the Poor, 22-23

Thus when we give we always receive. We give graciously. We receive graciously. We are not burdened by our service. We are freed. Freed from hurry and busyness. Free from accomplishment. Free from having to please others. Free to be with Jesus. The yoke indeed is easy, the burden light.

Looking Inward

1. Are you confident of your standing with God? What makes you confident? What robs you of that confidence? How does that confidence affect your service to others?

2. When you meet someone in need, is your first reaction to avoid them? To help them? To pray? Should prayer be our first reaction? Why or why not?

3. What discourages you most as you serve others? What practices can help you overcome that discouragement?

4. Do you find it easier to serve or to be served? Do we need to learn how to accept service? What might teach us?

Try This Week

1. Make a list of all the people you regularly help and serve. This might include particular church ministries in which you serve, but should reach beyond those ministries. For a week, pray daily for everyone you serve and every ministry you are involved in.

2. Make a similar list of all the people who have helped you in the last week. Daily pray for them.

Tools to Help

For deep, rich, and profound thoughts on restful service, see Thomas R. Kelly, *The Eternal Promise* (Richmond, IN: Friends United Press, 1966).

For practical spiritual guidance on compassion ministries, Robert D. Lupton, *Compassion, Justice, and the Christian Life: Rethinking Ministry to the Poor* (Ventura, CA: Gospel Light, 2007) is quite helpful.

We cannot become more like Jesus by self-effort or sheer imitation of Christ. We will fail. But we can follow another WWJD: Walking with Jesus Daily. We can with the help and empowering of the Holy Spirit, walk with Jesus daily by spending time with him in prayer, Bible reading and meditation, worship, solitude and silence, and other spiritual disciplines. As we abide or remain in him in the sweet communion of his transforming friendship, he will change us and mold us to become more like him. It is the Holy Spirit (Eph. 5:18; 2 Cor. 3:18) who will transform us, conforming us into the image of Christ (Rom. 8:29), or forming Christ in us (Gal. 4:19).

Siang-Yang Tan, *Full Service: Moving from Self-Serve Christianity to Total Servanthood*, 29

CONCLUSION
THE UNHURRIED LIFE

Now that you have finished this book, you might think, "That was good. I have a few new things to think about."

If that is your reaction, you missed the point of the book. This book is not meant merely to prompt discussion or thought. It is all about doing. If you "finished" the book in a few days or a few weeks, then the book did you little good. This is not about a book, but about your life. "Finishing" takes a lifetime.

The Jesus Way of Life

Each chapter of this book has focused on Jesus. He habitually lived in ways that opened his heart to the work of God. In a busy life, he made time for solitude and silence. He practiced simplicity. He enjoyed Sabbath. He served with the wisdom and strength God gave him. Go back often and look at those Jesus stories. God means for us to live like Jesus. What would Jesus do?

Each chapter also has a brief story of people who follow Jesus. These are not super-spiritual Christian heroes, but ordinary people like us. But God works mightily in ordinary people.

Christ in Us

What connects our lives to the life of Jesus? The practices of Jesus. Solitude. Silence. Simplicity. Sabbath. Service. Each of these is a point of contact between our lives and his life.

This is much more than merely imitating Jesus. It is impossible to be Jesus on our own! It is impossible to follow his practices based on our own determination. Even if we are dedicated and motivated! If we try the practices merely through our own strength, we will fail miserably. If we just try harder, the practices will be burdens, not an easy yoke.

But these practices are not about trying, but trusting. We do not try to do what Jesus would do. We will fail. But the great good news is that Jesus lives in us. His powerful presence through the Holy Spirit empowers us in the practices of Jesus. We imitate Christ because he lives in us.

So you are not through with this book. Or rather, it is not through with you. If you have not already, go back and begin. Begin small. Begin in trust. Make time to be alone with God. Add simplicity to solitude. Practice the gift of Sabbath. And you will find God at work in you in ways you cannot imagine. He will serve others through you, in a restful, unhurried, joyful life.

Trust. Practice. Follow.

> If you were to ask me point-blank: "What does it mean to live spiritually?" I would have to reply: "Living with Jesus at the center."
>
> Henri Nouwen, *Letters to Marc about Jesus: Living a Spiritual Life in a Material World*, 7

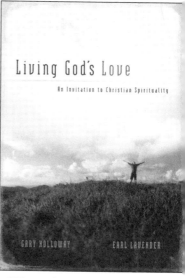